CHAINED BY FOOD

Marginalized Voices from Peri-Urban India

Community Perspectives in Environment and Development

No. 1 : Alternative Perspectives on Livelihoods, Agriculture and Air Pollution — Agriculture in urban and peri-urban areas in a developing country

—Neela Mukherjee

No. 2 : Perspectives of the Silent Majority: Air Pollution, Livelihoods, and Food Security—Indepth studies through PRA methods on community perspectives

—Amitava Mukherjee

No. 3 : Hunger: Theory, Perspectives and Reality

—Amitava Mukherjee

No. 4 : Chained by Food: Marginalized Voices from Peri-Urban India—Poor Households as Food Producers and Consumers in Peri-Urban India

—Neela Mukherjee and Meera Jayaswal

About the Authors

Dr. (Ms.) Neela Mukherjee is currently a development practitioner, researcher, trainer and a consultant to international development agencies such as UN-IFAD, UNDP, UNOPS, UNCDF, Asian Development Bank, NORAD, DFID, EC and others. She has long years of experience and professional standing as a development expert for her innovative and inter-disciplinary approach towards people-centered development in many developing countries including India, China, Vietnam, Sri Lanka, Bangladesh, Cambodia, Nepal, Laos, Maldives, Botswana, Ghana and Zimbabwe. Her major areas of interests include participatory and sustainable developmental practices, people-centered project design and methodologies, PRA-based micro planning, participatory monitoring and impact assessment, gender issues and sustainable livelihoods' practices. Formerly, a Professor of Economics at the LBS National Academy of Administration Mussoorie and an alumna of the London School of Economics and Political Science, she has written extensively on the subjects of her interests. Her books include the following:

1. *Alternative Perspectives on Livelihoods, Agriculture and Air Pollution — Agriculture in urban and peri-urban areas in a developing country*, (2001) SOAS Studies in Development Geography, Ashgate Publishing Co., U.K. and Concept, Delhi.
2. *Participatory Learning and Action with 100 Field Methods* (2002), Concept, Delhi.
3. *Participatory Appraisal of Natural Resources* (1997), Concept, Delhi.
4. *Questionnaire Survey & Participatory Rural Appraisal* (1995), Concept, Delhi.
5. *Participatory Rural Appraisal, Methodology and Applications* (1993), Concept, Delhi.

Dr. (Ms.) Meera Jayaswal is a Doctorate in Psychology and is an experienced field researcher in participatory approaches and has been associated with many development research projects in India. She is a PRA practitioner and has a large number of research publications to her credit. Apart from writing research papers she has co-edited *Learning to Share* – Volume I by Concept Publishing Company and co-authored *Alternative Perspectives on Livelihoods, Agriculture and Air Pollution — Agriculture in urban and peri-urban areas in a developing country*, (2001) SOAS Studies in Development Geography, Ashgate Publishing Co., U.K. and Concept, Delhi. Her other research interests include tribal health, education and reproductive health. She has conducted field studies for DFID's Livelihood Scoping Study in West Bengal and also undertook extensive fieldwork for CARE India's Concurrent Effect Assessment of Super Cyclone rehabilitation project in Orissa supported by DFID.

Community Perspectives in Environment and Development-4

CHAINED BY FOOD

Marginalized Voices from Peri-Urban India

Poor Households as Food Producers and Consumers in Peri-Urban India

NEELA MUKHERJEE
and
MEERA JAYASWAL

CONCEPT PUBLISHING COMPANY, NEW DELHI-110059

Cataloging in Publication Data—DK
Courtesy: D.K. Agencies (P) Ltd. <docinfo@dkagencies.com>

Mukherjee, Neela.

Chained by food : marginalized voices from peri-urban India : poor households as food producers and consumers in peri-urban India / Neela Mukherjee and Meera Jayaswal.

p. cm. — (Community perspectives in environment and development ; 4)

Study conducted in Faridabad District of Haryana and Varanasi District of Uttar Pradesh, India.

Includes bibliographical references (p.)

Includes index.

ISBN 8180692388

1. Food chains (Ecology)—India—Faridabad (District). 2. Food chains (Ecology)—India Varanasi (District). 3. Vegetable trade—India—Faridabad (District). 4. Vegetable trade India—Varanasi (District). 5. Food consumption—India—Faridabad (District). 6. Food consumption—India—Varanasi (District). I. Jayaswal, Meera, joint author. II. Title. III. Series: Community perspectives in environment & development ; 4.

DDC 577.160 954 558 21

This study is based on a project funded by the United Kingdom Department for International Development (DFID) (Crop Post Harvest Research Programme), project number R7530, led by Dr. Fiona Marshall (f.marshall@ic.ac.uk), Imperial College of Science, Technology and Medicine, London). The views expressed are not necessarily those of DFID.

Dr. Neela Mukherjee was the team leader for the participatory component of the Project on "Food Quality Assurance" conducted by Development Tracks in Research, Training & Consultancy Company, New Delhi. Dr. Meera Jayaswal was a senior member of the core team involved in field research.

ISBN-81-8069-238-8

First Published 2006

Published and Printed by
Ashok Kumar Mittal
Concept Publishing Company
A/15-16, Commercial Block, Mohan Garden,
New Delhi-110059 (INDIA)

Phones : 25351460, 25351794
Fax : 091-11-25357103
Email : publishing@conceptpub.com

PREFACE

This study was funded by DFID's Crop Post Harvest Research Programme, London. This was the participatory field research component of a larger research project "Enhancing food chain integrity quality assurance mechanisms for air pollution impacts on fruit and vegetable systems". The participatory field research component of the project was led by Dr. Neela Mukherjee along with Dr. Meera Jayaswal and a team of field researchers.

The peri-urban farmers in India play a critical role in the food chain for supply of food to those residing in cities and towns of India. Livelihoods of poor households in the peri-urban India are strongly dependent on growing vegetables and cereals and selling them in near-by towns and cities. Though seldom recognized, the small and marginal cultivators play a critical role in the food chain for supplying a steady stream of perishable items such as vegetables—spinach, cauliflower, okra and other vegetables and milk to the city dwellers. They constitute the backbone of a city's food supply system, in this case Delhi—a mega city and the capital city of India and the city of Varanasi—a major business hub and tourist attraction in the State of Uttar Pradesh. It is in this context that participatory action research was undertaken in 15 peri-urban villages in the two Indian states of Haryana and Uttar Pradesh located in the North. The study is based on listening and learning from the voices of the poor producers and consumers of food from the peri-urban areas of India during the period 2000-2003.

The main aim of the field research was to learn from the poor groups of crop/vegetable producers and the consumers in the peri-urban areas about their food growing and consuming practices, as well as their institutional context, and to draw policy inferences based on such research. The field research based on participatory rural appraisal (PRA) methods specifically examined the underlying issues as follows:

- What role horticulture produces (especially, spinach, cauliflower and okra) play in the livelihood strategies of poor producers?
- What food do poor people consume in their households? Do poor women have different perspectives on food consumption as compared to that of poor men?

- What are the livelihood options of poor households as producers of food?
- What vulnerabilities do they face in producing and consuming such food?
- What are the related production and consumption practices and their coping strategies?
- What types of "food safety" practices do the poor producers have as food growers?
- What types of "food safety" practices do the poor have as food consumers?
- What are the problems/constraints, impacts, challenges and opportunities faced by the poor producers and consumers of food?
- What kind of roles do the local level institutions play in terms of information, advice and support system for livelihoods of poor producers and consumers?
- What are the implications of the field results in terms of policy and practice?

Field inquiry was located in different sites in the Indian states of Haryana and Uttar Pradesh. In Haryana, the sites were located near the industrial hub of Faridabad in the peri-urban areas where agriculture practices continue with the extension of the "green revolution" belt from the rural Haryana. Though Faridabad is an industrial belt, vegetables and good quality grains produced in the peri-urban areas are located near the main roads within 5 to 8 kilometers. The people living in the peri-urban areas of Faridabad pursue two major sources of livelihoods—agriculture and livestock raising. They are faced with major vulnerabilities in terms of industrial pollution, which is affecting their agriculture and health. Acquisition of land for urbanisation by Haryana Urban Development Authority (HUDA) is directly impacting on their traditional livelihoods. Various factors such as rapid urbanization, mushrooming of industrial units, non-adhering of pollution standards, vehicular pollution, etc. are lending adverse impact on quality of life, agricultural production and livestock rearing, both directly and indirectly.

In Uttar Pradesh, Varanasi is a major city with agriculture being practised in its peri-urban areas. As far as Varanasi is concerned, it is a major market city having extensive marketing networks, both by road and rail, far and wide across the state and the country. It is also a tourist city attracting large volume of tourists from rest of India and abroad. It has agricultural fields located in its peri-urban and rural areas. In Varanasi, the peri-urban areas are fertile and productive and cater to essential vegetable supply to the city and elsewhere. Though Varanasi is not considered as a district located in the core area of green revolution belt of India, its agriculture and horticulture production provide livelihoods to millions of land-owners and daily labourers.

Being the hub of marketing activities, vehicular pollution is a major impediment to quality of life and the city is also not free from industrial pollution, especially pollutants from local industries producing Banarasi sarees, ornaments, toys, leather goods etc. Its peri-urban areas have direct benefits from proximity to urban markets for selling agriculture produce and milk. The present study focuses on aspects of food quality and safety for selected vegetables – cauliflower, spinach and okra—from the perspectives of both producers and consumers in the peri-urban areas.

Key Research Findings

1. Those people living in the peri-urban areas of Faridabad near the industrial belt pursued two major sources of livelihoods—agriculture and livestock-raising. They were faced with major vulnerabilities in terms of industrial pollution, which was affecting their agriculture and health. Acquisition of land for urbanisation by Haryana Urban Development Authority (HUDA) was directly impacting on their traditional livelihoods.
2. In the study villages of both Faridabad and Varanasi many small and marginal farmers cultivated vegetables, either as a main source of livelihood or as support towards crop cultivation. Most vegetables grown were sold in the market and only leftovers were consumed. Farmers tried to get the maximum amount possible from the crop cultivated. Farmers were cultivating vegetables for commercial purposes due to their proximity to markets in urban areas.
3. Spinach, okra and cauliflower were all sold in the market. They received equal amounts of income from harvesting of both spinach and cauliflower but production of cauliflower was much higher as compared to spinach. However, from their health point of view, spinach was considered to have medicinal properties. Apart from the summer crop, spinach was harvested four times a year and was less labour-intensive when compared to the eight varieties of cauliflower grown by many farmers.

Findings from Peri-Urban Villages – Faridabad

Role of horticulture practices in local livelihoods

4. In the peri-urban areas of Faridabad, different income groups cultivated different vegetables as determined by their land size/socio-economic status. Large farmers (with land holdings of more than five acres) preferred cultivating foodgrains while small farmers (with

land holdings up to two acres) preferred vegetable cultivation as they got better income from the vegetables and found it easier to manage their livelihoods for the whole year. The medium size farmers (with land holding between two to five acres) mainly cultivated winter vegetables to supplement their income from the main crop.

5. Cultivating vegetables in the field was primarily for income generation. Many horticulture producers cultivated different types of vegetables round the year. Those with more working hands preferred vegetable cultivation to those with less working hands. The farmers preferred family labour for vegetable production in order to reduce cost.
6. Vegetable cultivation required more farm inputs in comparison to paddy and wheat and yielded more income but involved higher risk. Profit was dependent on the right price of the vegetables in the market though marketing was not easy in some villages due to the distance involved in approaching local markets.
7. Vegetable production was one of the principal means of livelihood for the *Sainis*. However, for other caste groups—*Pundits*, *Ahir*, *Jat* and *Gujar*, it was a means of supplementing income.
8. Vegetable cultivation was continuing for the last thirty years because of its increased demand in the urban areas. With establishment of new factories, rapid urbanization and rising health consciousness demand for vegetables had increased sharply.
9. The risks of producing cauliflower were many. It was easily damaged by hot and cloudy weather and in case of fall in market prices due to excess supply, there was little or no profit or even net loss. For the last five years, the risks in cauliflower cultivation had increased manifold, hence the cultivators were replacing cauliflower with potato cultivation.
10. The risk of cauliflower production to damages inflicted through bad weather and pests was the maximum as compared to growing spinach and okra. For okra it was the minimum. The marginal landowners avoided cauliflower cultivation because of such risk involved, which could lead to wiping out their source of livelihood or induce high vulnerability.
11. Okra had high returns but its cultivation was expensive. Moreover, large land was needed for such high returns. Hence, small and marginal landowners did not prefer okra.
12. Spinach was the most preferred vegetable for those with less land including the medium landowners (having less than two acres of land). Many *Saini*'s cultivated spinach because it required regular labour. All family members of *Saini* worked hard for high returns.

13. Spinach was being grown not only by small farmers but also by medium farmers. For the last five years, the income from spinach had increased due to the increased demand. People's awareness about spinach was increasing as a vegetable good for health.
14. The involvement of men, women and children in vegetable cultivation varied by the income level and caste group.
15. The *Saini* women from all income groups were involved in cultivation activities. Their men purchased seeds and other materials from the market and also went to markets for selling vegetables. The women from other caste groups were involved in vegetable cultivation though not as much as the *Saini* women. The *Pundit* women were more conservative and less involved in vegetable cultivation. Most of their men supervised the daily labourers employed for vegetable cultivation.
16. Most of the horticulture produce was sold in the wholesale market. Only a few cultivators were retailers. In Faridabad, the vegetables were usually sold in the Ballabhgarh wholesale market. If supply was in excess of demand, market prices tended to fall. The middlemen in the markets played an important role in fixing price. The producers were vulnerable for they had no say in fixing price of their own horticulture produce.
17. Many were aware of the nutritional value of vegetables though most households belonging to the big farmers did consume them on a regular basis. But for the poor households they depended mostly on consumption of wheat and rice.
18. Most women were aware that spinach was good for health and pregnant mothers were required to consume it for healthy growth of foetus. Since most women did not get to eat spinach, they consumed other green leaves that they could get. Apart from this, many households with homestead sowed spinach for home consumption.
19. Only a few rich farmers and those who faced shortage of manpower produced horticulture items like guava etc.
20. About 40 years back cultivation of barley, millet, pearl millet and horse gram was in practice but slowly the trend shifted in favour of paddy, wheat and vegetables such as carrot, radish, spinach, okra, cauliflower, etc. for commercial purposes.
21. All cereals were first stored for household consumption and only the surplus amount was sold in the market for procuring other essential items. In case of vegetables and horticulture produced by small and marginal farmers they were mainly sold in the market to procure cereals.

22. Vegetables were sold up to 98 per cent of production and a minor portion was used for household consumption and as gifts to relatives. The latter also included vegetables, which were damaged and could not be marketed. There was high investment in vegetables by those engaged in vegetable cultivation and their livelihoods were dependent on it.
23. Though the produce was sold in the market there was no organized marketing or cooperative. The farmers sold individually in Faridabad and competed with each other. In this bargain they often failed to get their cost price. At the start of the season, the vegetables were sold for good price but the prices tended to fall towards the end of the season. Lack of cold storage facility also reduced the chance of storing vegetable produce for long.
24. Though men were recognised as farmers and cultivators, women actually invested more time in fieldwork in addition to their household work. The men groups either went off to work as labourers or spent time in playing cards. Women had more information regarding pest attack on vegetables, diseases and on patterns of crop growth. Even children were involved in different agricultural activities.

Pre- and post-handling of selected vegetables

25. Horticulture producers as part of pre-harvest handling of the produce took some precautions. These included giving adequate time gap between use of pesticide and marketing of vegetables. All vegetables were washed after being harvested to make them look clean and attractive and then packed to be sold in the market.

Types of information and support systems

26. There was little or no institutional support for the promotion of horticulture produce. During serious damage and loss from vegetable production, the cultivators arranged loans from moneylenders in the village or the businessmen of the town. Only a few *pundits* could manage loans for agriculture.
27. For the type of farm inputs the farmers were dependent on their past experience and notes exchanged with other farmers. For the new varieties they consulted mainly the local shopkeeper/trader selling agriculture inputs. Such informal consultation mainly related to seed varieties, fertilisers and pesticides. The farmers rarely approached the local agricultural research station—the Krishi Vigyan Kendra (KVK).

28. The poor farmers could access crop information through radio and discussions in the village. However, the local shopkeepers of pesticides/agro-inputs was the major source of advice.
29. The farmers felt the need for proper information dissemination. They suggested that priced booklet should be made available at the seed shop. The booklet should contain information about best practices for profitable cultivation, marketing, information on funding agencies for getting soft loan etc.

Food preparation and consumption practices

30. Consumers were aware of food safety issues mainly related to use of fertilizers and pesticides rather than impact of air pollution from the industrialised belt of Faridabad. Some group members were of the opinion that air pollution had no impact on vegetable cultivation but affected their health causing breathing problem and other diseases. Few others were of the view that air pollution impacted on plants as well.
31. Some individual farmers revealed that they injected medicine in pumpkin and brinjal plants to increase their size and weight so as to fetch better market price. They said that they were not sure of the adverse impact of such vegetables on consumer health. Such farmers always preferred local variety for self-consumption and grew separate plants for home consumption.
32. Most often customers were not aware of safety aspects of food in terms of vegetables. Food safety was not much of a concern in case of cooked food items. The consumers went by fresh look of the vegetables as well as the price.
33. Consumption of raw vegetables by consumers was limited to a few items such as cucumber, tomato, carrot and radish. Some took them while working in the fields. All vegetables were mainly taken in the cooked form. Children consumed raw items much more than adults.
34. In the village, the people were aware that horticulture items and vegetables were needed for strength of the body and for protection against different diseases. About perceived nutritional value, spinach, carrot and radish were considered the best amongst the vegetables in the village. Cauliflower, cabbage and okra were considered as city vegetables – which did not provide much strength to the consumers.
35. Consumption of seasonal vegetables along with cereals was considered most essential. People from the study villages did not perceive much nutritional value of cauliflower and okra as compared

to spinach. The belief that cauliflower and okra created flatulence in the stomach was shared by the participants from all study villages.

36. Some pregnant women had the opportunity to learn from the ANM (trained mid-wife), who visited the village and asked them to take green vegetables such as spinach for strong eyesight of would-be children.
37. The nutritional value of selected vegetables did not affect the choice of vegetables grown. It was mostly determined by the size of land holdings of individual farmers. If the land area was relatively large, the cultivators were ready to take the risk of cultivating cauliflowers.
38. In the study villages all the vegetables and green leaves were first cut and then washed.
39. Most of the villagers consumed few vegetables. They usually consumed locally available vegetables, preferably from their own land. Even poor villagers preferred to manage vegetables from cultivators free of cost. Only *pundits* ate relatively higher quantity along with a variety of vegetables throughout the year.
40. The vegetables were cooked with a large amount of chilies, much oil and spices. None of the villagers consumed filthy vegetables. When vegetables became filthy, they were fed to the livestock or thrown away.
41. The awareness about impact of chemical inputs in agriculture was low amongst many villagers. The impact of increased doses of pesticides, fertilizers, pests, dust and smoke emitted from near-by factories were not perceived as inflicting much of damage to human health.
42. There was no institutional mechanism in existence for dissemination of correct information in relation to consumption of unsafe food and its health hazard. Whatever information the villagers gathered was ad hoc and limited.

Findings from Peri-Urban Villages—Varanasi

Role of horticulture practices in local livelihoods

43. Majority of peri-urban villagers in the sampled villages cultivated few vegetables for livelihood purposes as well as for home consumption.
44. Caste groups had a close correlation with the cultivation pattern e.g., Rajbhar were not used to cultivating cauliflower because they considered it as a tedious job. The Moryas and Patels cultivated six varieties of cauliflower, which involved considerable hard work.

45. The perceived nutritional contents of the vegetable produced did not influence the cultivation patterns. Spinach, tomato and carrot were perceived as having maximum nutritional content as compared to cauliflower and okra though production of the latter group of vegetables was considerable.
46. The income from cauliflower was high despite the expenditure on insecticide and risk of damage. Such income was invested in major household expenditure e.g. repayment of loans, arrangement of marriage, house repair, purchase of livestock, etc.
47. The cultivation of selected horticulture produce increased since the last 15-20 years. Usage of inputs – fertilizer, insecticide, etc. also increased due to loss in soil productivity and increased resistance of insects to insecticides.
48. Much of the horticulture produce was sold in the wholesale market/s. The *Arhatia* was the middlemen who sold the produce to wholesalers. He took five to six per cent of the amount received from the cultivator in terms of small amounts of vegetables. Some vegetables were also sold on a retail basis.
49. Usually the men carried the horticulture produce to the wholesale market, by bus or bicycle. They started their journey to the market by 6 to 7 a.m. in the morning and returned by 10 to11 a.m. The margin of profit of the cultivator was more in the retail markets although the time consumed for selling vegetables was higher as compared to the wholesale market.
50. More than 96 per cent of the produce was sold in the market and less than 5 per cent of the produce was kept for personal consumption and as gifts for relatives.

Pre- and post-handling of selected vegetables

51. The use of chemical fertilisers was increasing steadily. The villagers did perceive the adverse impact of increased fertilizer use on soil productivity as well as on the quality of crop/vegetables. However, they were unable to take action in absence of viable alternatives. Application of insecticides to vegetables was on the rise.
52. The women were mostly of the opinion that use of fertilizer and pesticide harmed human health. Moreover, application of fertilizer reduced the nutrient content of the soil.
53. After application of pesticide hands were washed though not properly. The household members—the head of the household, the wife and the children—were involved during spraying of pesticides. The pesticide residual was not perceived as dangerous.

54. The women believed that one or two proper wash reduced the impact of residues.
55. The sprayed vegetables were sold in the market on the day following the application of pesticides.
56. The vegetables were harvested and sorted out by the family members. During the process of harvesting, neither the human hands nor the instruments were washed and sanitized. The harvester spat and urinated on one side. There were pet dogs, which usually roamed freely in the vegetable land. The women did not find any contamination effect.
57. Spinach, after harvesting, was spread on the ground or on jute bags/ *bora*. Such bags were not washed for the purpose of eliminating contamination.
58. The villagers, men as well as women groups were aware of vegetables getting exposed to dust. But they believed that those were not the sources of contamination. The primary belief of villagers was that stale food was unsafe food.
59. Cauliflower was considered unsafe if there were too many pests, its colour had become pale and flowers tended to become loose.
60. The effect of dust due to vehicular traffic was perceived to be harmful only in case of okra. For spinach and cauliflower, such dust could be removed by washing. The toxic effect of vehicular pollution was not perceived at all.
61. The vegetables were consumed only in those months when they were locally available from their own land. Even the high-income groups rarely purchased vegetables (except potato) during off-season from the market for daily use. During off-season, vegetables were purchased at a high price by the better offs only for their guests. The low-income groups did not usually consume vegetables during the off-season. There were no significant differences in the pattern of consumption of vegetables in the urban and peri-urban areas of Varanasi.
62. For poor households, vegetables were usually consumed in the evening while pulses were consumed in the morning. The amount of per head consumption of vegetables was very low e.g. half a kg of cauliflower/okra was enough for a family of six members, parents and four children.
63. In the urban area studied, the children of five years or under, both boys and girls, did not consume vegetables. They also did not have any liking for vegetables. The adult men and adolescents consumed more vegetables and the elderly members of the family did the same. The elderly had a preference for spinach followed by cauliflower and okra. No one ate raw vegetables as done in the peri-urban areas.

64. The method of washing and cooking was not conducive to sanitizing or nutritional preservation. Spinach was washed before cutting the vegetable because its leaves were perceived to be dirty. Okra was washed before cutting it into pieces so that its juice did not ooze out. Cauliflower and other vegetables were washed before cutting them into pieces. There was no concept of water-soluble nutrients.
65. The vegetables were prepared according to traditional cooking and food habits. The cooked vegetables were spicy and tasty, cooked in reasonable oil. Two much oil was not used by poor households due to paucity of cash.
66. Usually cow-dung was the fuel used for cooking vegetables. Poor households who did not own livestock bought cow-dung cakes or wooden dust for cooking. They were not aware of any detrimental effect of heat on vegetable nutrient.

Washing and cooking habits of the villagers and exposure to food contamination

67. Vegetables were not washed properly. The cutting instruments were also not washed prior to cutting. The village women thought that the purpose of washing was to remove soil. There was little or no awareness about contamination of food.
68. Washing of hands before handling food was not prevalent. Children were not encouraged to wash hands before eating. The cooked food was not covered properly.

Existing information and support system for horticulture producers

69. For horticulture practices the only source of information was the local seed shop and/or the pesticide shop. There was no support system for production of selected horticulture produce. Similarly, there was no source for acquiring information on food safety and nutrition. Information source related to preservation of nutrients by improving washing and cooking methods was also non-existing.

Policy inferences and recommendations

70. Some factors affecting small/marginal vegetable producers and consumers are agricultural constraints, infrastructural constraints, marketing constraints, lack of suitable institutional support , lack of access to network/information, policy changes for rapid urbanization, industrial pollution, low literacy, lack of awareness on food safety practices and lack of women's empowerment.

71. The recommendations include reducing vulnerabilities; stabilizing market prices of vegetables; not planting vegetables during off-season to reduce risk; reducing vulnerabilities by growing new types of crops; enabling empowerment through information dissemination and other measures as described below.
72. Institutional support is required for strengthening the capacity of the small and marginal producers of vegetables in the peri-urban areas.
73. Some policy do-ables for strengthening production of vegetables by small and marginal producers include:

    (i) Demonstration/pilot schemes at the local level in the peri-urban areas will help in propagating good and efficient practices for vegetable cultivation.

    (ii) Large scale propagation of integrated pest management techniques, compost-making methods, and organic cultivation practices for producers would ultimately support food safety practices.

    (iii) Making available enough water for irrigation, especially for those growing vegetables in the peri-urban areas;

    (iv) Making available financial support to promote local horticulture, especially for small and marginal horticulture producers, whether through banks or cooperatives.

    (v) Making available agricultural inputs such as seeds and fertilizers at fair price and on a regular basis for sustainable agriculture.

    (vi) Raising awareness for improving food safety practices including sanitation practices for better handling of vegetables and preventive health aspects.

    (vii) Information base available with the local fertilizer/pesticide shop could be strengthened. Information brochures along with other literature and interactive multi-media facilities could be made available at such contact points.

    (viii) Vegetable producers could be encouraged to form vegetable farmers' cooperatives and their institutional linkages could be strengthened with service providers such as input suppliers, banks, extension agents, marketing networks and others.

    (ix) The government could support market intelligence network and flow of other relevant information for vegetable producers.

    (x) Development of markets and brand name for organic vegetables will help in creating niche market areas. Value additions could be undertaken through downstream processing of vegetables and provisions for preservation/packaging of sliced vegetables and their trade.

(xi) Raising awareness in nutrition and promoting health education and knowledge amongst women.
(xii) Demonstration sessions will help to promote better cooking practices for preservation of the nutritive value of the vegetables.

74. On the consumption side, selected initiatives are required from the governance side to promote food safety practices in vegetable consumption.
75. Establishment of food processing enterprises should be encouraged as an integral aspect of national policy with appropriate incentives. Establishment of storage facilities like godowns along with cold storage could also be set up at different locations in consultation and collaboration with horticulture producers.
76. Setting up of proper drainage facilities for channeling polluted water and its treatment should constitute essential part of the industrial units and flouting of anti-pollution laws should be properly tackled.
77. Future directions of field research could include exploration of information needs of small and marginal farmers and setting up of information networks and preparation and dissemination of educative audio-visual materials on food safety practices and related issues.
78. Field findings indicate that the impacts of air pollution and water pollution are interrelated. Water as a source of pollution is more visible to the farmers than air as a source of pollution. Hence, in order to have a complete picture on food safety it is important to conduct further field research on impacts of water pollution on vegetable production and its interrelationship with air pollution.

The book provides an integrated picture of issues related to poverty, agriculture, small and marginal produces and consumers, urbanization process, food safety and food security in peri-urban India. Based on field findings in peri-urban belts of Haryana and Uttar Pradesh, the book presents the perspectives of the farmers, both as producers and consumers on the role of agriculture, food production and consumption practices, quality of life and the effectiveness of institutional support networks available to them. It captures the views of key social stakeholders to provide comprehensive and balanced analysis of major issues in peri-urban agriculture facing India today. The findings highlight the pivotal role peri-urban agriculture plays in societal and cultural aspects such as gender, health and food safety as well as the traditional concepts of livelihoods, employment and income. In featuring the issues related to poverty, food safety and livelihoods as an agricultural, economic and societal concern, this book is one of the pioneering books available in the field.

This book is of direct relevance to development practitioners, development agencies, agricultural professionals, NGOs, environmentalists, urban planners, international and national development agencies, students of environment and development studies, researchers in the area of poverty and environment and policy makers.

The topic of food in peri-urban areas is a research frontier. As far as our knowledge goes, no book is currently available on the linkages of peri-urban poverty with food safety issues. Hence, there is little basis available for comparison. However, we may add that unlike most previous studies the book presents the perspectives of the farmers themselves (the primary stakeholders in agriculture) on the role of agriculture, food production and consumption practices, urbanization and industrialization, quality of life and the effectiveness of their existing support networks.

CONTENTS

GLOSSARY OF INDIAN TERMS

Aganwadi	A government child welfare day care centre where children up to the age of 5 receive free food and health check up.
Arhatia	Middleman
Baithak	Living room
Bajra	A coarse cereal
Banga	Disease afflicting buffaloes. It affects the feet and it gets swollen.
Baroo	A type of weed which looks similar to jowar and is found mostly in jowar fields.
Barsam	Fodder sown in winter.
Basti	Ward or colony in a village organized mainly on the basis of caste/religion.
Bathua	A weed
Bigha	Measure of Land: 5 Bigha = 1 acre
Biswa	Measure of Land: 5 Biswa = 1 acre
Burela	Another name for caterpillars
Cauliflower	*Phulgobhi* (Local term)
Chapattis	Roti (*Local term*)
Chaumasa	Four months
Chepa	Tiny white insects—suck juice out of leaves of cabbage, bajra, mustard and sugarcane leaves. Has a sticky texture.
Chhedak	Any caterpillar that bores holes. It is also called Dhola/Burela
Chitli	A worm that eats vegetable roots
Chula	Oven or stove made out of mud which uses wood, animal dung etc. as fuel.
Chutney	Prepared from green/dry chillies, garlic and salt
Congress Grass	A weed having small white flowers. Also called Parthenium

Coriander	*Dhania* (*Local term*)
Dhencha	Medium sized fodder plants sown in summer.
Dhola	Caterpillars that bore holes
Fatinga	Any pest which is a grasshopper
Galagotu	Disease found in buffaloes. It chokes buffaloes to death
Gander	A general term for caterpillars
Gram Samiti	A village co-operative society
Gram Sewak	An appointee of the Block Development office for supervising development work in the village. He/she looks after 3 villages
Gurchawa	A disease which results in wilting and crippling of leaves
Hara Kira	Small green caterpillar
Harwawa	A disease which turns leaves yellow
HUDA	Haryana Urban Development Authority
ICDS	Integrated Child Development Scheme
Jhansi	A cluster of small caterpillars (pest)
Jhulsa	A disease resulting in wilting and blackening of leaves
Jowar	An inferior cereal used as fodder now
Jute bag	*Bora* (*Local term*)
Kanduwa	A disease which affects the ear-rings of wheat and turns them black
Kasba	A village which is the centre of rural growth having a population of 7000 or more
Kateli	A medium sized tree-weed having thorns
Katui	A pest which cuts down paddy ear-rings
Kilas	Acres
Kirona	A caterpillar
Koria	Crippling of leaves and plants like a leper The fruits of the affected plants look deformed
Kundi	Water reservoir
KVK	Krishi Vigyan Kendra
Lalrii	Red coloured small sized pests which can fly It eats leaves of leafy vegetables

Machchi/Makhi	House-fly
Mandi	Wholesale market
Morya or Gurchawa	A disease which wilts and cripples leaves especially in chilies and tomatoes
Moti mala	Bead necklace
Muhalla	Wards/Colony
Najla	Ailment: running nose, headache, nose burning
Nakshatra	A constellation
Nilagai	Blue bull
Okra	*Bhindi* (*Local term*)
Pankhi	Any pest which can fly
PRA	Participatory Rural Appraisal
Pradhan/Sarpanch	Village head, usually elected to the village level unit of governance
PRRA	Participatory Rapid Rural Appraisal
Rani Jai	A weed similar in looks to wheat and whose seeds are like wheat grains, though slightly black in colour
Safed Moondi	A weed having small seeds (coriander type), mainly found in wheat fields
Sambar	A kind of deer
Sati	Small sized weeds which mainly grow in bajra fields
Soondi	Small sized caterpillar found in paddy leaves It sucks the sap
Spinach	*Palak* (*Local term*)
Telchatta	Small sized pest which can fly It sucks juice out of mustard pods and cauliflower
Tidḍa	A current variant of locust which is small in size
Tiddi	Large sized locust (the earlier variant)
Tikuli	A beetle that sucks juice from leaves of vegetables mostly found in summers
Titri	A small white moth which sucks milk from paddy ear-rings

LOCAL MONTHS TO ENGLISH CALENDAR

Baisakh	Mid-April to mid-May
Jeth	Mid-May to mid-June
Asar	Mid-June to mid-July
Sawan	Mid-July to mid-August
Bhado	Mid-August to mid-September
Kuwar	Mid-September to mid-October
Kartik	Mid-October to mid-November
Aghan	Mid-November to mid-December
Poosh	Mid-December to mid-January
Magh	Mid-January to mid-February
Fagun	Mid-February to mid-March
Chet	Mid-March to mid-April

1

INTRODUCTION

Two states of India—Haryana and Uttar Pradesh—were selected for researching on food safety where one district from each state was focused upon for fieldwork. The two districts were Faridabad district in Haryana and Varanasi district in eastern Uttar Pradesh. Both the districts were the ones where the earlier DFID project on air pollution and agriculture crop yield was located. Hence the present project enabled continuation of earlier rounds of field research in the same two districts for better understanding of farmers' perspectives and this time on food production practices, quality and local livelihoods of poor farmers.

Faridabad, an industrialised hub in the state of Haryana, is surrounded by "green revolution" belt in its peri-urban and rural areas. Those people living in the peri-urban areas of Faridabad (the focus of this study) near the industrial area pursue two major sources of livelihoods—agriculture and livestock raising. They are faced with major vulnerabilities in terms of industrial pollution, which is affecting their agriculture and health. Acquisition of land for urbanization by Haryana Urban Development Authority (HUDA) is directly impacting on their traditional livelihoods. Various factors such as rapid urbanization, mushrooming of industrial units, non-adhering of pollution standards, vehicular pollution, etc. are adversely impacting on quality of life, agricultural production and livestock rearing, both directly and indirectly.

As far as Varanasi is concerned, it is a major market city having extensive marketing networks, both by road and rail, far and wide. It is also a tourist city attracting large volume of tourists from rest of India and abroad. It has agricultural fields located in its peri-urban and rural areas. Though Varanasi is not considered as a district located in the core area of green revolution, its agriculture and horticulture production provide livelihoods to millions of land-owners and daily labourers. Being the hub of marketing activities, vehicular pollution is a major impediment to quality of life and the city is also not free from industrial pollution, especially pollutants from local industries producing Banarasi sarees, ornaments, toys, leather goods, etc. Though there are direct benefits from proximity to urban markets for selling agriculture produce and milk, the impact of industrial pollution on agriculture productivity is not a mean impact to ignore. This was the subject of our earlier study on "Community perspectives on air pollution and agriculture crop yield". The present study focuses on the aspects of food quality and safety for selected vegetables—cauliflower, spinach and okra—from the perspectives of both producers and consumers in the urban and peri-urban areas.

Though Faridabad and Ballabhgarh are industrial belts, vegetables and good quality grains are produced in the peri-urban areas located near the main roads and within five to eight kilometers from main roads. Similarly, in Varanasi, the peri-urban areas are fertile and productive and cater to essential vegetable supply to city and elsewhere. The field inquiry was undertaken to look at food safety practices of producers and consumers of vegetables and the impact of environmental pollution on horticulture produce in the study villages.

1.2 FIELD RESEARCH—OBJECTIVES

The main aim of the field research was to learn from the perspectives of local women and men on food safety practices and livelihoods-related issues based on participatory methods. The underlying issues guiding field research were as follows:

- As producers and consumers of food, what are the local communities' (gender) perspectives on food safety and food security?
- How are such perspectives related to vulnerability, coping strategies and sustainable food-livelihood aspects and the factors determining them?
- What are the related practices, problems/constraints, impacts, challenges and opportunities?
- What kind of roles the local level institutions play in terms of food quality assurance and livelihoods sustainability?
- What are the implications for policy and practice?

1.2.1 Specific Objectives of the Fieldwork

(i) To understand the role of selected horticulture produces (spinach, cauliflower and okra) in the livelihood strategies of urban and peri-urban poor.

(ii) To study the food preparation and consumption practices among the urban and peri-urban poor.

(iii) To understand the existing information, advice and support system for horticulture producers.

(iv) To understand the existing advice, support and information, which are available to urban and peri-urban consumers.

1.2.2 The main aim of the field research was to learn from the perspectives of the local women and men on what they grow and eat and the food safety practices that they adopt and their institutional linkages, if any, as producers and consumers. The field research based on Participatory Rural Appraisal (PRA) methods specifically examined selected issues as follows:

- What role do the horticulture produces (especially spinach, cauliflower and okra) play in the livelihood strategies of the poor producers?
- What food do poor people consume in their households? Do poor women have different perspectives from poor men?
- What vulnerabilities do they face in producing and consuming such food?
- What are the related production and consumption practices and their coping strategies?
- What types of "food safety" practices do the poor producers adopt as food growers?
- What types of "food safety" practices do the poor have as food consumers?
- What are the problems/constraints, impacts, challenges and opportunities faced by the poor producers and consumers of food?
- What kind of roles do the local level institutions play in terms of information, advice and support system for livelihoods of poor producers and consumers?
- What are the implications of the field results in terms of policy and practice?

1.2.3 In the above context some relevant social issues addressed during field research are listed below:

- Were the poor more likely to be *producing* a disproportionate amount of contaminated vegetables—why and to what extent? What were the elements of production that could affect the extent of contamination?
- If there were interventions to ensure safety what impact it could have on poor producers?
- Were the poor more likely to be *selling* a disproportionate amount of contaminated vegetables—why and to what extent? What were the

elements of marketing that could affect contamination? If there were interventions to ensure safety what impact it could have on poor producers?

- Were the poor likely to be *consuming* a disproportionate amount of contaminated vegetables—why and to what extent? What were the elements of purchasing, preparation and consumption patterns that affected the degree of contamination that various groups were exposed to?
- This would lead them to a set of policy recommendations and suggestions for affected communities to find out what type of interventions could be made to improve the safety of the vegetables that are produced, marketed and consumed.

Based on fieldwork in two states of India—Haryana and Uttar Pradesh—in Faridabad and Varanasi districts respectively, the study aimed at learning from peri-urban producers and consumers about issues related to food quality and livelihoods. The fieldwork was a combination of both exploratory and topical approaches to peri-urban areas through application of PRA methods where nine and six peri-urban villages/municipal areas were covered in Faridabad and Varanasi, respectively.

2

LIVELIHOOD STRATEGIES AND HORTICULTURE PRODUCERS—FARIDABAD

Faridabad, an industrialised hub in the State of Haryana, is surrounded by a "green revolution" belt in its peri-urban and rural areas. Those people living in the peri-urban areas of Faridabad (the focus of this study) near the industrial area pursue two major sources of livelihoods — agriculture and livestock raising. They are faced with a major vulnerability in terms of industrial pollution, which is affecting their agriculture and health. Acquisition of land for urbanisation by Haryana Urban Development Authority (HUDA) is directly impacting on their traditional livelihoods. Various factors such as rapid urbanization, mushrooming of industrial units, non-adhering of pollution standards, vehicular pollution and other agriculture and infrastructure constraints are adversely impacting on quality of life, agricultural production and livestock raising, both directly and indirectly. Though there are direct benefits from emerging urban markets for selling agriculture produce and milk, the impact of industrial pollution on agriculture productivity is not a mean impact to ignore. This was the focus of DFID's earlier collaborative study between 1997–99 on air pollution and agriculture crop yield. The present study focuses on food quality and safety-related issues for selected vegetables—cauliflower, spinach and okra from the perspectives of both producers and consumers in the peri-urban areas of Faridabad and Varanasi.

Four rounds of field inquiry were conducted to find out the impact of air pollution on vegetable cultivation in the peri-urban areas of Faridabad lying in and around the industrial belt. The study covered nine villages. Though Faridabad and Ballabhgarh are industrial belts, vegetables and cereals are produced in the peri-urban areas including those situated near the main roads and in those within five to eight kilometers from main roads. For selection of hamlets in different villages considerable care was taken for comparing different hamlets within any selected village and studying those hamlets, which grow more vegetables. The approach to the village groups in the villages was in terms of interacting with farmer groups who cultivated vegetables and those who also consumed them. The timings for the meetings were decided by the farmer groups. Interactions with the sample group/s were held on a random basis. In some cases during transect walk, separate discussions were held with individual farmers growing vegetables in their fields. Separate group discussions were held with women groups in order to flag gender issues.

The names of the study villages are as follows:

(i) Unchagaon
(ii) Chandawali
(iii) Machchgar
(iv) Malerna
(v) Sahupura
(vi) Sahapur Kalan
(vii) Sumper
(viii) Badoli and
(ix) Budhayna.

Of the total households in the above peri-urban villages, majority of them are engaged in agriculture and livestock rearing. The landless work as labourers in fields, industrial areas and in other places. Vegetable cultivation in the study villages differs in terms of background of the cultivators. For example, in many villages, including Budhayna, the local farmers are engaged in cultivation of vegetables, whereas, in village Badoli, the migrants cultivate them by leasing land from local landowners. Though vegetables are grown in all the study villages, the volume of production differs widely amongst the villages, including those of cauliflower, okra and spinach. The vegetables produced are marketed in Faridabad, Ballabhgarh, Badarpur and Okhla. They are transported to near-by markets on bicycles/bus etc. and to distant markets by vans/trucks, depending on the volume of produce to be transported. The water facility for cultivating vegetables, though reasonable with most cultivators having tube-wells, is threatened by the rapid fall in water table and the polluted water in the vicinity of the industrial belt of Faridabad.

2.1 ROLE OF HORTICULTURE PRODUCE AND LIVELIHOODS STRATEGIES

Local communities in the peri-urban areas of Faridabad pursue a range of livelihoods. They include the following:

- Cultivation of cereal crops,
- Cultivation of vegetables,
- Agriculture labour,
- Rearing milch animals,
- Government jobs,
- Private sector jobs,
- Shop keepers, and
- Others.

2.2 CULTIVATING DIFFERENT VEGETABLES

Farmers in the study villages cultivate different vegetables including cauliflower, okra and spinach though their proportions vary. For instance, in village Unchagaon, around 25 per cent of the population comprises of small farmers and another 25 per cent is landless. These farmers lease land from either the government or big farmers. On half the land so acquired, shorter crops such as spinach, coriander, methi, bathua, pudina, etc. are cultivated and in the other half, in the winter season, cauliflower, potato, carrot, etc. are grown. In summer, this is substituted by kankri, bitter gourd (karela), tomato, turai (gourd), chilies, pudina, etc. In rainy season, chilly, kachri, okra, ghiya, turai, spinach, etc. are grown while on the skirts of the field; radish, chukander etc. are planted. In case of villages such as Malerna, Sahupura and Sahapur Kalan, vegetable cultivation is only 10 per cent of total cultivation though in village Sumper it is 60 per cent as shown in Table 2.1.

In the study villages many farmers cultivate vegetables, either as a main source of livelihood or as a support towards crop cultivation as shown in Table 2.1. Most vegetables grown are sold in the market and an insignificant part is utilised for home consumption. Farmers try to get the maximum amount possible from the crops cultivated. Farmers are cultivating vegetables for commercial purposes due to their proximity to different markets and also due to the village being located near roadside. The fresh green vegetables can be reached to the market easily and are principal sources of livelihoods for many households. For others, it is mainly for home consumption that vegetables are grown in small patches in their homestead. The vegetables grown in the peri-urban areas of Faridabad are many including cauliflower, brinjal, spinach, coriander, methi, cucumber, lady's finger and others.

Table 2.1: Faridabad—Vegetable Cultivation and Livelihoods: An Overview

Peri-Urban Hamlet/ Village in Faridabad	*Vegetable Cultivation as Source of Livelihood*	*Approximate No. of Households growing Vegetables and doing other activities*	*Approximate Area under Vegetable cultivation as proportion of total cultivable area*
(1) Village Unchagaon,	High	Total Number of HH –845 Vegetable cultivation Daily labour	Total cultivable land: 600 acres Seasonal vegetable cultivation: 80 per cent
(2) Village Chandawali,	Medium	Total Number of HH – 795	Total cultivable land: 2400 bigha. Out of the total agricultural land, 60 per cent is utilized for vegetable farming, 30 per cent for mix of vegetable and wheat and 10 per cent for cattle feed, barsam, jawar, etc.
(3) Village Majhgar	Low	Total Number of HH – 260	Total cultivable land: Not available
(4) Village Malerna	Low	Total Number of HH – 350 People in agriculture: 50 per cent	Total cultivable land: 500 acres Vegetable cultivation: 10 per cent
(5) Village Sahupura	Low	Total Number of HH – 350 People in agriculture: 45 per cent	Total cultivable land: 650 acres Vegetable cultivation: 10 per cent
(6) Village Sahapur Kalan	Low	Total Number of HH – 163 People in agriculture: 70 per cent	Total cultivable land: 400 acres Vegetable cultivation: 10 per cent
(7) Village Budhayana	High	Total Households – 412 Vegetable cultivation (35 HH) General cultivation (248 HH) Daily labour – (90 HH)	Total cultivable land: 352 acres Cauliflower – 69 per cent Spinach – 25 per cent

(Contd.)

(Contd.)

Peri-Urban Hamlet/ Village in Faridabad	*Vegetable Cultivation as Source of Livelihood*	*Approximate No. of Households growing Vegetables and doing other activities*	*Approximate Area under Vegetable cultivation as proportion of total cultivable area*
(8) Village Badoli	Very low	Total Number of HH – 431 General cultivation (320 HH) Vegetable cultivation done by a few (4) migrant HH	Total cultivable land: 422 acres Vegetable cultivation – Negligible
(9) Village Sumper	High	Total Number of HH – 320 People in agriculture – 50 per cent	Total cultivable land: 600 acres Vegetable cultivation: 60 per cent

Note: HH stands for households. Significance of vegetable cultivation as a source of livelihood is "high" if the proportion of cultivable land growing vegetables (okra + spinach + cauliflower) is more than 50 per cent. It is "medium" if such proportion is below 50 per cent but above 30 per cent. It is "low" if it is below 30 per cent.

Box 1: Displaced Households in Unchagaon—Land Acquisition by HUDA

Around 25 per cent of the population of Unchagaon are landless labourers. Out of this, 15 per cent households are engaged in cultivating land acquired on lease. HUDA has acquired 90 per cent of village land. Earlier, there was intense agricultural activity in the village, mainly vegetable cultivation and therefore labour was required for eight months in a year and on average, 20 days in a month. Now the available agricultural land is dwindling in size and the scope of gaining livelihoods is diminishing. In the month of Baishakh (April-May), when wheat crop is reaped, there are opportunities for daily work. At the same time, there is work in vegetable fields, thereby giving double remuneration to the labourers. Premwati, Phulwati, Munni and Chatra are some of the women who depend on such remuneration. They can provide for education of their children up to primary level but there is no scope for further studies. These women work mostly in fields and have a lot of experience about vegetable cultivation.

Source: From the field notes of Saraswati.

2.3 WHY GROW VEGETABLES?

The farmers in the peri-urban areas of Faridabad grow vegetables for cash income, for supporting livelihoods, for wage employment, for self-consumption, for health purposes and some also use the plant residue as fuel (that of okra). Spinach, okra and cauliflower are all sold in the market. They receive equal amounts of income from harvesting of both spinach and cauliflower but production of cauliflower is much more compared to spinach. However, from their health point of view spinach has medicinal properties. Apart from the summer crop, spinach is harvested four times. It is less labour-intensive as compared to the eight varieties of cauliflower cultivated by many farmers.

2.4 VEGETABLE CULTIVATION AND LAND OWNERSHIP

Cultivating vegetables, whether for subsistence or for income generation depends on the size of land holding of a household. One can trace a proximate relationship of the type of vegetables grown with size of land holdings of different socio-economic groups. Different socio-economic groups tend to cultivate different vegetables as determined by their land size/socio-economic status as illustrated in Table 2.3. Large landowners (with land over five acres) prefer cultivating cereals such as paddy, wheat and oilseeds like mustard. They also cultivate potato as a cash crop though its fluctuating price in the last few years has been quite discouraging for the farmers. Those with adequate manpower prefer cultivating vegetables to those with less working hands. The farmers prefer family labour for vegetable production since employment of outside labour for vegetable fields leads to more cost and little or no income.

Small and marginal farmers (land holding up to two acres) prefer cultivating vegetables, which are relatively more remunerative and help them to manage their livelihoods for the whole year. While the medium-sized farmers (land holding between two to five acres) cultivate only winter vegetables to supplement their income from the main crop. Their preferred vegetables are potato, carrot and cauliflower. Farmers, generally cultivate two types of vegetables—one in winter and the other in summer. The winter vegetables require less water and, hence, are preferred by the farmers.

2.5 SEASONALITY OF VEGETABLE CULTIVATION

Green vegetables are planted more in the summer season starting from the month of Baishakh to Kuwar run up-to the month of Kartik. Mixed crop is also planted in the rainy season. Radish is planted on spaces bordering the fields. In the winter season, cultivation of methi, spinach, dhania is the highest. An illustration is given in Table 2.2 from village Unchagaon of a small farmer, who produces different vegetables round the year together with some foodgrain and fodder.

Table 2.2: Seasonal Cultivation of Agricultural Land

<table>
<tr><th>Month</th><th colspan="2">Vegetable grown</th><th>Foodgrains-wheat, jwar, jai, barsam</th></tr>
<tr><td>Chait</td><td colspan="2">Vegetable 80 per cent - preparation of field</td><td rowspan="2">20 per cent - Foodgrains wheat, jai, barsam</td></tr>
<tr><td>Jeth (at present)
Asar
Sawan
Bhadon</td><td colspan="2">ghiya, turai, okra, kankri, bitter-gourd, tomato, chilly, onion, pudina, spinach</td></tr>
<tr><td>Kuwar</td><td>Prepare field</td><td>Ploughing etc.</td><td></td></tr>
<tr><td>Kartik
Aghan
Poos
Magh
Fagun</td><td>cauliflower</td><td>spinach, dhania, methi, carrot, chukander, radish</td><td>Potato</td></tr>
</table>

Village: Unchagaon, Dated: 19-03-2001, Field researcher—Saraswati

2.6 CULTIVATING CAULIFLOWER

In the peri-urban areas of Faridabad, some farmers at least grow eight varieties of cauliflower. Of them, the Aghani and Push varieties are good with big flowers and least insects. Cauliflower is cultivated since 10-12 years and the crop is fully dependent on chemical fertilizers and pesticides. Cauliflower is grown mostly for selling in the market, to prepare seeds, for self-consumption, to use leaves as fodder and to offer as gift to relatives and friends. Although cauliflower gives high yield at low cost, there are practical constraints faced by the producers. Chepa is an insect that affects the cauliflower crop and causes total damage. Infected cauliflower cannot be fed even to livestock. Lali is another insect that affects cauliflower crop but is less destructive than Chepa. Gider insects get inside the flowers and cause harm. Peacocks damage the crop by getting into fields and eating the flowers. Monkeys also cause harm by not only eating the flowers but also damaging it.

2.7 GROWING SPINACH

It is mainly consumed in winter. Very few farmers grow spinach. The small and marginal farmers have some land, which women generally care for. The men buy fertilizers and pesticides from the market when required and also sell the spinach. Production of spinach is mostly for commercial purposes suitable for households with small land size. Such production engages many family members. A small part of the production is consumed by households and the leftover is also fed to livestock. Farmers, having more than one *kila* (acre) of land, cultivate vegetables like tomato, cauliflower and okra on a large scale. In large-sized cultivation of such vegetables, the role of women is equal to that of men.

2.8 GROWING OKRA

Okra has good yield in many villages though not all farmers grow it in a big way. Two varieties of okra—indigenous and hi-breed—are grown. Even with modern inputs, the indigenous variety does not give high yield whereas the hi-breed okra crop sown in June yields high production by October-November. The okra production, if sustained for two months, costs Rs. 5,000 in terms of inputs and fetch returns worth Rs. 15,000. The second crop can be harvested after a short time. The subsequent crops generally yield net profit of Rs. 10,000 to Rs. 15,000 per kila (acre). Okra is grown mainly for commercial purposes and its return is high. Producer households consume only a small part of okra while its stems are dried and used as fodder. For hi-breed okra, the crop sown in June is ready within 42–60 days. By August-September, the produce can reach the market. After September the plants stop yielding for a month but the plants re-branch and start growing fresh okra. This is again ready to be harvested in about two months time. At the beginning, okra crop requires much care and attention together with doses of medicines and fertilizers.

Box 2: How to Cope with Falling Prices?

In village Sumper most households depend mostly on vegetable cultivation as main source of their livelihoods. In village Sahupura, the farmers revealed that actually vegetable cultivation fetches more profit only if one is able to do it. In the past years the price of major crop like rice has collapsed significantly from Rs. 968 per quintal in 1999 to Rs. 805 quintal in 2000. Wheat prices have also fallen from Rs. 759 per quintal in 1998 to Rs. 605 per quintal in 2000. Such falling price trend has disappointed farmers and, now, most are in favour of cultivating vegetables. However, in the past years potato prices have also declined. So the farmers are of the opinion that a balanced cultivation of cereals and vegetables is a better option, given access to essential inputs such as water, power etc.

Source: From the field notes of Bratindi Jena.

2.9 GROWING VEGETABLES AND COMMUNITY PREFERENCES

The peri-urban villages have different communities living in them such as Saini, Jat, Gujjar, Dalit, Yadav and others. In addition to crop cultivation, many households cultivate vegetables such as cauliflower, spinach, okra, potato, tomato, chilly, brinjal, cucumber, kankri, coriander, methi, pudina, radish, etc. However, not all communities cultivate vegetables. The Sainis cultivate spinach, methi, coriander, radish, chukander and cauliflower as they have considerable experience in cultivating vegetables. Their entire families thrive on vegetables grown on small sized land. Despite difficulties in cultivation of okra, many Dalit households cultivate this crop. The vegetable growers in Jat community derive ten times more profit from cultivation of chilly despite long gestation period of this crop. They also cultivate potato. The Gujjars pursue extensive cultivation of tomato.

2.10 SELLING VEGETABLES AND MIDDLEMEN

The farmers sell the vegetable produce in the market, however, not at their price but at market price dictated by the traders/middlemen/commission agents in the markets. These agents come empty handed to the market and in the span of a few hours, buy vegetables from the villagers at a low price and sell them at higher price. They also earn commission from both the villagers as well as the buyers. This gives them a huge margin of profit at the cost of the toil of the farmers. Some of the younger people of the villages have learnt the tactics from the commission agents and started similar activities. Rohtash Singh is the first person from Majhgarh village to begin this work. He arrives from the village to the market empty hand and in five hours time earns about Rs.15,000 per month. In busy seasons, such earnings can go up to Rs.20,000.

2.11 WORLDVIEW ON VEGETABLE CULTIVATION

Sometimes cultural practices work against vegetable cultivation. For instance, in village Badoli, vegetable cultivation is looked down upon. In this village, migrant workers from east Uttar Pradesh and Bihar grow vegetables. Such temporary residents of the village lease land, construct their temporary huts near the field and cultivate vegetables. The means of livelihood of the permanent residents are completely different from that of the migrant population. The permanent residents of the village consider their traditional occupation of livestock rearing and milk production as better option and also a matter of pride. They consider vegetable cultivation as an occupation low in dignity as compared to rearing of milch animals. For them, selling vegetable is a matter of shame. They are also of the view that milk production involves less labour than vegetable farming. Vegetable cultivation requires more hands, time and labour in comparison to milk production, which can be supplemented along with other activities without much extra effort. Also in terms of returns, the average net earnings per day in milk production with one buffalo is Rs. 55 and a household is easily able to rear four buffaloes at a time thus taking the net earnings to Rs. 220 per day. In comparison to this, vegetable cultivation in one acre yields Rs. 72 per day after deducting all costs, which is lower than that of milk production, given the labour involved.

The migrant group in village Badoli grows cauliflower, spinach, cucumber, gourd and turai while okra, coriander and methi are grown on a smaller scale. Cultivation of vegetables by the migrants is a source of livelihood, bringing profit and also supporting self-consumption. In village Badoli, highest return is from cauliflower and several varieties of cauliflowers are grown and sold. Spinach cultivation is cheaper than cauliflower and the crop grows well but market is limited. Hence, from the viewpoint of livelihoods, growing cauliflower is a better option. Spinach is therefore cultivated on less land as compared to cauliflower. Cauliflower is grown on 4.5 acre, which is 1.06 per cent of total agricultural land. Spinach is grown on 1.75 acres of land which is 0.41 per cent of total agricultural land. Okra is grown on about one acre of land which is 0.23 per cent of total agricultural land.

2.12 GROWING VEGETABLES IS NOT EASY

There are also instances where some households tried to cultivate vegetables but failed due to inexperience. For example, 25 Gujjar families in Chandawali village tried their hands in vegetable cultivation on the land they owned. Their traditional livelihood is buffalo rearing and they were trying to adopt a new source of livelihood i.e., vegetable cultivation. They tried cultivating brinjal, chilly, potato, onion, okra, cauliflower, etc. but failed due to inexperience. They incurred continuous loss for some years and discontinued cultivation of vegetables. Land got fragmented due to distribution amongst the community members. The Gujjar families no longer cultivate cauliflower, okra and spinach for their livelihood but buy it from the market for self-consumption. They utilise their land to grow animal fodder such as jowar, jai and barsam crops. In case some households cultivate vegetable, it is only brinjal, tomato, potato and chilly.

2.13 SEARCHING ALTERNATE SOURCES OF LIVELIHOODS

Of late, many villages engaged in agricultural activities and livestock rearing in the peri-urban areas have started looking for alternate sources of income due to problems/constraints faced. One practical problem is the acquisition of land by the Haryana government, which has de-stabilised traditional livelihoods of farmers and many households have been affected in the process. Alternative avenues of employment are being sought in government and non-government jobs, though not so easily available. Some also work as vehicle drivers after completing their education.

2.14 ECONOMICS OF COSTS, OUTPUT AND INCOME — VEGETABLE PRODUCTION

Based on the views of farmers from the peri-urban areas of Faridabad, vegetable cultivation requires relatively more inputs and labour compared to paddy and wheat. Though such production yields more income, it also involves higher risks. In case the market price is remunerative then it is possible to earn profit from each variety of vegetables grown. For the interior located villages marketing is not that easy due to the distance involved and hence vegetable cultivation is relatively less lucrative, given transport cost/constraint. Different vegetables are cultivated by different groups of farmers based on their land size.

2.15 ECONOMICS OF CULTIVATING SPINACH

It is generally the small and marginal farmers who own one or less than one acre of land who grow spinach all throughout the year. High yield is possible in respect of spinach with less cost and more effort. After sowing spinach on a small sized land, daily efforts are required. Spinach cultivation is done all round the year. One crop cycle lasts for three to four months. The threat of losing crop is the least for spinach except for ginder (pest) infestation. Removing the infested leaves and feeding animals take care of this problem. New leaves of spinach grow easily.

Two varieties of spinach are cultivated, namely, *Shish* (with stems) growing more in summer and *Sada* (without stems) grown in the winter. The crop runs for four months and can be cultivated in all seasons. The crop is almost ready in a month and can be sold after the 42nd day. In winter (October to February), the yield of spinach is good. In rainy season (June to September), the crop requires extra sprinkling of medicines as insects multiply during this season. During the summer months between February to May, the sale of spinach comes down except for wedding receptions when spinach is used as one main item of feast. Table 2.3 provides an illustration of spinach cultivation and related activities from village Unchagaon.

The medium farmers with land holding of five acres cultivate bigger vegetables along with smaller ones like spinach/methi/dhania, which require more labour. The number and type of vegetables to be cultivated depends on the number of members in that concerned household. For example cultivation of spinach requires more labour and is therefore not done by small sized families. Further if spinach is cultivated on a large area, the resultant high supply of spinach in the market brings down prices and reduces profits.

Table 2.3: One Crop Cycle of Spinach: Income-Expenditure and Activity – Unchagaon [One Kila (acre) of Land]

Month	*Activity*	*Expenditure (in Rs.)*	*Income (in Rs.)*
Bhadon	Preparing the field	500	–
Kwar	Sowing spinach	500	–
Kartik	Draining and adding fertilizer	200 500	–
Aghan	Draining, carrying product to market	200	5,000
Paus	Draining, carrying product to market	200	5,000
Magh	Draining, carrying product to market only up to half the month	200	2,000
Fagun	Preparing for the next crop	–	2,000
	Total		**14,000**

Village: Unchagaon, Dated: 18-03-2001, Researcher: Saraswati

Large farmers (with land holding of more than five kilas) in Faridabad from Saini caste cultivate shorter crops on small area of land and longer duration crops on large area of land. The relationship of land size to vegetables is illustrated from village Chandawali. In this village as shown in Table 2.4, those with more land plant less vegetable and use it mostly for home consumption except commercial crops such as potato. Those households with less than two bigha of land mainly grow fodder. While those households having land between three to five bigha grow mainly wheat and potato, some fodder and little vegetable for home consumption. Those with land over two acres grow mostly wheat and potato, some spinach for home consumption and a range of vegetables including cauliflower and okra.

There are various constraints to vegetable cultivation, in terms of pest attack, attack by stray animals, lack of irrigation facility and labour shortage. There is not much support available to overcome such constraints. Often due to blue bull attack the entire crop, b th vegetable and foodgrain can get damaged. During winter, pest attack damages cauliflower crop. There is high competition in the market and damaged vegetable get low price for the buyer prefers good variety. The farmers are at the receiving end in terms of prices obtained. Given the fragility of vegetables and difficulties in stocking it, often the buyer bargains for a price, which is actually a loss to the farmer. Still they prefer to sell their produce at a lower price since they cannot carry it back to their village.

Table 2.4: Ratio of Vegetable to Foodgrains' Cultivation, Chandawali

Land fit for agriculture	*Total HH*	*Wheat*	*Potato*	*Spinach*	*Okra*	*Cauli-flower*	*Fodder/ Other Vegetables*
Less than two bighas	30	–	–	–	–	–	Fodder- Barsam, Jawar Jai
Three to five bighas	30	2 bigha	3 bigha	–	Some for home consump-tion	–	Fodder- Jawar, Barsam
Two to three acres	40	2 acres	1-1/2 acres	Some for home consump-tion	Three bigha	Three bigha	Vegetables- Cucumber Chilly Brinjal Tomato
More than 4 acres	30	3 bighas	4 acres	Some for home consump-tion	2 per cent for home consump-tion	1 bigha Some for home consump-tion	Vegetables- Cucumber Gourd Chilly Turai Brinjal

Note: HH stands for households.
Source: From the field notes of Saraswati.

Irregular electricity supply is a major constraint to vegetable cultivation. As per the farmers, they do not get enough electricity for cultivation while the hotels in Faridabad waste electricity on neon signs and pompous decorations. This makes the farmer communities feel discriminated against the urban lobby in terms of meeting their basic needs. Alternative to electricity is oil but increasing price of oil is also discouraging in terms of cultivation.

2.16 ECONOMICS OF CULTIVATING CAULIFLOWER

Most farmers cultivate cauliflower because of high yield and as a good source of livelihood. In the absence of any natural calamities, yield from cauliflower goes up to Rs. 10,000 to Rs. 15,000 on a total cost of Rs. 4,000, thereby giving net return between Rs. 6,000 to Rs. 11,000. However, for the last four-five years, cauliflower crops are earning losses continuously and it has become difficult even to retrieve the cost. In the year 2001, the entire crop was afflicted by checha and was damaged. Such damaged crop could not be fed even to livestock. The field had to be re-ploughed without harvesting since that would have added to farming cost.

Box 3 : Story of Lekhram Selling Cauliflower

In village Unchagaon, there is good cultivation of cauliflower. Lekhram Saini from the village sells vegetables in retail market. Lekhram sells the vegetable from his own field. People buy his vegetables because they are fresh. He sells the stale vegetables at lesser price and the poor buy such vegetables. He helps his family in fieldwork from the morning to afternoon, after which he takes the fresh vegetables to his shop in the market. However, for the last four-five years, there has been continuous loss in cultivation of cauliflower and to meet the household expenses. Five years ago, with this income, life would run smoothly and he could afford to eat wheat, gram, jowar etc. The income would be sufficient to meet expenses on his children's education, electricity bills and other daily needs. In 1982, the cauliflower crop sown in the months of Magh-Pausa (January to March) was ready when hailstones fell and the entire crop was destroyed. Not even one cauliflower was spared. This was a big loss and to meet the loss, Lekhram took loan from the moneylender to purchase seeds and fertilizer. The next crop was sown after two months and the loss was made up.

Source: From the field notes of Saraswati.

Farmers in peri-urban Faridabad cultivate eight varieties of cauliflower as follows:

(i) First Yearly
(ii) Kuari
(iii) Katki
(iv) Aghani

(v) Phoosi
(vi) Mahia
(vii) Bilayati
(viii) Sonoball

First Yearly cauliflower is cultivated in the months of Baishak and Jeth (April to June). The crop, being not seasonal, costs more and often more afflicted by insects due to heat. First Yearly variety gives higher yield than others. In the case of indigenous cauliflower, the seeds are sown in the fields and plants are grown. At the outset the field is ploughed and fertilizers added before seeds are sown. Expenditure is incurred on ploughing, mixing and on purchase of fertilizers. The saplings are prepared from the seeds sown in one's own fields. Cow dung (*gobar*) is also used along with chemical fertilizers, otherwise the yield gets affected. The crop requires several rounds of watering. The crop is ready in about one and a half months time. The farmers have past experience and plant different varieties in different parts of their fields. Cauliflower crop is a traditional crop, which has gradually come to depend on fertilizers. The more the use of fertilizers, the higher is the yield. One constraint is multiplication of *ginder* insect.

Table 2.5: Comparative cost and returns from Spinach, Cauliflower and Okra

(in Rs. from one acre of land)

	Spinach	*Cauliflower*	*Okra*
Income – Unchagaon	14,000	20,000	20,000
Income – Majhgarh	–	12,000	20,000
Income – Chandawali	20,000	19,000	20,000
Cost – Unchagaon	3,000	5,000	5,000
Cost – Majhgarh	–	4,000	5,000
Cost – Chandawali	4,000	7,000	7,000
Net Returns – Unchagaon	11,000	15,000	15,000
Net Returns – Majhgarh	–	8,000	15,000
Net Returns – Chandawali	16,000	12,000	13,000

Note: Collated from field notes on Faridabad villages.

2.17 ECONOMICS OF CULTIVATING OKRA

Both men and women farmers were of the view that the yield from okra cultivation is high and does not require much labour and is not fraught with much risk. However, only 10 per cent of the farmers cultivate okra. One constraint in cultivating okra, as gathered from discussion, is that, there is much labour involved in picking okra from plants and that there is risk of injury to the hands from the thorny okra plants. The 10 per cent of farmers who cultivate okra said that more cost is involved at the beginning for ploughing and sowing the crop. Later, some amount is spent on pesticides. The okra crop produces yield continuously for four months.

Table 2.6: Comparison of Risks, Yield and Costs in Cultivating Vegetables

	Okra	*Spinach*	*Cauliflower*	*Potato*
High cost	: : 4	.. 2	: : : 6	: : : : 8
More medicines	: . : 5	: . 3	: : : 6	: : . 5
High nutrition	.. 2	: : : : : 10	.. 2	.. 2
High risk	: : 4	: 2	: : : 6	: : : : 8
More fertilizers	: : 4	: : 3	: : . 5	: : : 6
Good taste	: : : . 7	: : : 5	: : . 5	: : : . 7
More gider	: . : 5	: . 3	: : : : 8	None
More insect attack	: : 4	: . 3	: : 4	: : . 5
Cause flatulence	: : : . 7	0	: : : . 7	0
Cause heat	0	: : : 6	0	: : 4
Need more water	: : . 5	: : : 6	: : . 5	. 1
High yield	: : : : . 9	: : . 5	: : : 6	: : : 6
Difficulties	: : : : . 9	: : : 6	: : 4	: . 3

Village: Unchagaon, Dated: 19-03-2001, Researcher: Saraswati

Note: This is matrix scoring done by village women with 10 as the highest score and 0 as the lowest score.

Table 2.5 gives a comparative picture of costs and returns from the three vegetables under consideration – spinach, cauliflower and okra – on one acre of land from three peri-urban villages in Faridabad – Unchagaon, Majhgarh and Chandawali. The table shows that spinach has the highest return as compared to the other two vegetables. Table 2.6 provides a comparative scoring of four vegetables – okra, spinach, cauliflower and potato–based on different criteria such as cost, medicine, nutrition, risk, fertiliser applied, taste, gider attack, insect attack, flatulence, causing heat, water, yield and difficulties in production. Spinach scores relatively high on nutrition (score 10), causing heat (score 6) and needing more water (score 6), okra has high yield (score 9) and causing flatulence (score 7), cauliflower has incidence of gider (score 8) and flatulence (score 7) and potato is relatively high cost (score 8) and high risk (score 8) though good to eat (score 7).

In terms of actual cost, yield and net profit from five vegetables – cauliflower, okra, potato, chilly and spinach as shown in Table 2.7 data from village Chandawali shows that net profit is the highest in case of chilly at Rs. 45,000 per acre. This is followed by net profit from potato and spinach (Rs. 16,000 per acre).

Table 2.7: Cost, Yield and Net Profit from Cauliflower, Okra, Potato and Spinach (*in Rs.*) (*Land Unit 1 acre*)

Sl. No.	*Crop*	*Production/Risk*	*Cost*	*Income*	*Net Profit*
			Rs.	*Rs.*	*Rs.*
1	Cauliflower	Cauliflower reaches market by 42nd day, the flowers are soft so carrying is risky	7,000	19,000	12,000
2	Okra	Fear of insects & termite, crop runs for four months, higher yield with lesser costs	7,000	20,000	13,000
3	Potato	Less cost and more yield	14,000	30,000	16,000
4	Chilly	The chilly crop runs for ten months, the crop is ready in four months, if cultivated with onions then double profit	5,000	50,000	45,000
5	Spinach	The crop runs throughout the year	4,000	20,000	16,000

Dated: 8-04-2001, Village Chandawali, Faridabad.

2.18 PERSPECTIVES ON NUTRITION AND PRODUCTION CHOICES IN HORTICULTURE

In the peri-urban areas, many people are aware of the nutritional value of vegetables and those households with access to more land are in a better position to consume them on a regular basis, whether from their own field or by purchasing them. By and large, cultivation of vegetables is not influenced by nutritional content. It is rather influenced by the potential demand of a particular vegetable. If the market price of a particular vegetable is attractive then the cultivator plans to cultivate it in the following season. This leads to over-supply of that vegetable with many producers growing the same vegetable. The cultivators generally do not discuss what vegetables they intend to cultivate and also tend to hide the wrapper of vegetable seed so as to reduce the possibility of imitation by their fellow producers.

Poor households depend more on wheat and rice and prefer grain cultivation because they get food, fodder and fuel for the whole year. Not many poor households get to eat spinach, though many women from poor households are aware that spinach is good for health and also good for pregnant women. Spinach is believed to strengthen vision and improve eyesight. Some think that it heats up the body and if eaten in winter keeps the body warm. Even buffaloes produce more milk if fed with spinach. Many households with little land or homestead grow spinach for home consumption.

Most villagers are aware that consumption of cauliflower causes flatulence though they are not aware of the exact nutritional content of cauliflower. The farmers use not more than 15-20 per cent of their cauliflower crop for self-consumption. Although, the crop in full bloom and in good health is a beauty to behold, cauliflower cannot be eaten daily.

Those who like preparation of okra procure it from the market in those villages where okra is not cultivated. The poor households, however, go without okra due to lack of purchasing power. The farmers are not generally aware of the nutritional value of okra. Some think that because it is a green vegetable, it has some nutritional value. Okra causes flatulence also. Despite this many people, especially children, prefer to eat okra.

2.19 PRODUCTION PRACTICES AND TRENDS IN HORTICULTURE CROPS

About 40 years back farmers cultivated barley, millet, pearl millet and horse gram but gradually the trend shifted towards cultivation of paddy, wheat and vegetables — carrot, radish, spinach, okra, cauliflower, etc. There were shifts in terms of both type and quantity of crops produced. With land size dwindling over time vegetable cultivation gained significance and those types were cultivated which had high demand.

We have already indicated in section 1 about the inputs used in production of vegetables. As far as production practices from harvesting to marketing are concerned, some of the general steps followed are as follows:

- The vegetables — cauliflower, spinach and okra – are harvested one day in advance of sending them to the wholesale market.
- If the vegetables are to be transported to the retail market then they are harvested on the same day before noon.
- To look fresh, the vegetables are soaked in a small tank "*kundi*" for 10 minutes.
- In order to retain freshness harvested cauliflowers are covered with leaves.
- The men tie the vegetables to their cycle.
- The spinach is cut and tied into small bundles in the field.
- The wholesaler goes to the market around 5-6 a.m. while the retailer goes around 3 p.m.
- The middleman/trader quotes the price without weighing after observing the vegetables and guessing an approximate weight. The middleman favours purchaser because he gets a commission from the purchaser between five to eight per cent.

- The vegetable producer has no say in the price quoted by the middleman.

2.20 SOURCES AND TYPES OF ADVICE TO FARMERS IN HORTICULTURE

In all study villages, the farmers mentioned that regarding usage of agricultural inputs they go by the past experience. For new varieties they consult local shopkeepers/traders and sometimes the local Krishi Vigyan Kendra (KVK). According to the farmers, the local shop-keepers are often better informed than KVK. The farmers consult the shopkeepers mainly on seed varieties, fertilizers and pesticides used for different crops. Vegetable growers in the Pandit hamlet of village Chandawali usually meet agricultural officers/ personnel and consult them about new seeds, fertilisers and insecticides. They also consult the local traders in agriculture inputs and are more bothered about two vegetables—cauliflower and okra.

Regarding the type of information related to cultivation of vegetables, men are outward-oriented and generally tend to have more information relative to women, especially on the following aspects:

- High yielding seeds of cauliflower and okra,
- Chemical fertilizers,
- Appropriate vegetables to be cultivated,
- Amount of seeds and fertilisers to be applied on land,
- Techniques for repairing tractors, motors, sprayer, etc., and
- Trends in market price of vegetables.

Women were better informed on the following:

- When irrigation water is required,
- When weeding is required,
- When vegetables should be harvested for selling,
- Number of daily wagers required for performing different activities,
- How to harvest spinach most efficiently, and
- Timing of harvesting of various vegetables.

2.21 PROPORTION OF PRODUCE MARKETED AND/OR HOME CONSUMED

Marketing of cereals and vegetables differ widely. In case of cereals, they are first stored for household consumption and only the surplus amount is sold in the market for procuring other essential items. In case of vegetables, they are sold to the extent of 80 to 98 per cent while farmers manage household consumption retaining 20 to 2 per cent of vegetables. The return from vegetables also helps the farmer procure cereals.

2.22 SALE OF PRODUCE AND CHOICES

In the study villages, the farmers sell the horticulture produce individually, in the Faridabad market since there is no farmers' cooperative. At the beginning of the season, the farmers tend to get a good price but slowly the prices start falling towards the end of the season. At times, they are forced to dump their produce in the market and return almost empty-hand due to low price and inability to stock fragile vegetables. Lack of cold storage facility also reduces the chances of storing the produce for some time.

Nearly 95 per cent of the producers sell vegetable to the nearest market on a wholesale basis. Only five per cent of the vegetables get sold in the retail market. The wholesale market is relatively convenient because of less time taken to sell vegetables. The vegetable producers transport the vegetables to the market at about 6 a.m. and hardly spend an hour in selling them generally through middlemen. On the other hand, the retailer has to spend at least 6 to 8 hours in the market. In case all vegetables are not sold then he has to arrange some place to store unsold vegetables rented on a monthly basis. Hence, retail selling does not suit most vegetable producers because it is time consuming and inconvenient and hinder their engagement in other activities. The women believe in exchanging vegetables while men tend to think such exchange is a wasteful activity and prefer selling vegetables in the market.

2.23 HOUSEHOLDS IN MARKETING OF PRODUCE AND FOOD SAFETY

In all study villages, though men are formally recognized as being involved in land cultivation and all forms of agricultural activities, women actually invest more time in the field in addition to their household work. Women do most activities both at home and in the field and their workload is high. They do the entire work in fields in the absence of men. The men either go off to work as labourers or spend their time in playing cards. From cooking in their homes to working in the fields, even girls help their mothers as soon as they are 10 years of age. Women do maximum work in the vegetable field while men do the marketing of produce and control the income. Women have more information regarding pest attack, disease and also details of cultivation practices. Children are also involved in different agricultural activities. The women often take children to the field and they help their mothers in different activities, especially girl children.

Table 2.8: Village Chandawali — Jatwara — Gendered Roles in Agriculture

Occupation	*Women*	*Men*	*Children*
Ploughing	+	+	
Sowing	+	+	+
Preparing field	+	+	
Draining	+		+
Sprinkling medicines	+	++	
Fertilizer	+	+	
Watering	+	+	+
Harvesting	+		+
Washing vegetable	+		+
Bunching	+		+
Taking to market		+	

Source: From the field notes of Saraswati.

Table 2.8 on gendered roles in vegetable cultivation in village Chandawali shows that women are involved in all activities except taking the produce to the market, while men participate in draining, harvesting, washing and bunching of vegetables. Children are also engaged in many of the production activities. Table 2.9 shows how the women have no respite from household and fieldwork and are engaged in those activities, which are relatively time-consuming.

Table 2.9: Role of Men, Women and Children in Household and Agricultural Work

Activity	*Time*	*Women*	*Men*	*Children*
Cooking	4 hours	*		
Work	2 and 1/2 hours	**	*	*
Field ploughing	To supervise only		* with tractor	*
Field preparing	Whole day	*	**	*
Sowing seeds/plants	Whole day	**		*
Draining	Whole day	**		*
Watering	2-4 hours	*	**	*
Add fertilizer	1-2 hours		*	
Add medicines	1-2 hours		*	
Plucking/bunching	3-4 hours	**		*
Carrying to market	3 hours		*	*

Source: From the field notes of Saraswati; Dated: 17-03-2001.

About the method of washing selected horticulture produce, the first wash is done immediately after cutting/plucking vegetables from the field. The vegetables are washed in *kundi* (reservoir), which is located in/near, the vegetable field. The water in the kundi comes directly from the tube-well. After the first wash vegetables are sent to markets, both retail and wholesale.

Box 4: *Kundi* — A Water Reservoir

Kundi is a water reservoir in/around agricultural field, which serves several purposes such as for washing vegetables, for irrigation, for washing clothes, for bathing, for washing livestock, for soaking vegetables and washing them. On many occasions due to water stored in a kundi it develops moss on its cemented surface. The wall and surface look green. The villagers clean it with a broom and remove the moss, collected on its surface.

Source: From the field notes of Meera Jayaswal.

2.24 DEMAND OF POTENTIAL BUYERS FOR SAFE HORTICULTURE PRODUCE

The potential buyers are not aware of safe vegetables though freshness of the vegetables is a concern to many consumers. Food safety is a concern in case of cooked food items. It was mentioned that many consumers were mostly concerned about price and any vegetable available at a cheaper rate was preferred. The consumers generally demand the following as mentioned by the vegetable growers:

- Fresh vegetables,
- Crisp okra and fresh cauliflower,
- Naturally green okra and white cauliflower,
- Fresh spinach with green/tight leaves,
- Small tender okra,
- Small spinach leaves, and
- No insects in cauliflower and okra.

2.25 SUPPORT AND LINKAGES WITH EXTERNAL BODIES IN PRODUCTION ACTIVITIES

In case of all villages, agriculture traders/shop keepers and to a small extent the local Krishi Vigyan Kendra (only in very few villages) provide the farmers with any kind of support required for farming. There are no NGOs working in the area. The horticulture producers, both women and men, mentioned that there was little or no official support system in vegetable production and marketing. There was no information disseminated on the nutritional content of different vegetables. Local people though entitled to bank loans were reluctant to take them because of lengthy bureaucratic procedure and mortgaging of house/livestock.

2.26 PREFERRED INFORMATION CHANNELS

In case of peri-urban villages of Faridabad being close to Delhi, information channels are strong, especially for the rich farmers who are mobile having their own vehicle and are also well connected through telephone and TV. The poor farmers listen to radios and local discussions. The farmers prefer the advice of the local shopkeepers. For the peri-urban villages where HUDA is acquiring land such as Unchagaon the villagers were not sure whether they would be able to continue vegetable cultivation in future.

2.27 LEVEL OF AWARENESS OF PRODUCERS ON FOOD SAFETY AND STEPS TAKEN

In the study villages, the vegetable producers take some precautions for handling of produce. These include giving adequate time gap between use of pesticide and marketing of vegetables. All the vegetables are washed after being plucked and before being packed for transporting to markets. This makes them clean and attractive. Vegetable, which looks clean and fresh, gets better price as compared to its dull and dirty look.

In village Badoli, the producers mentioned the deficiencies in vegetables cultivated with sewer water. The vegetable-growers informed that 10 years back, sewer water used for vegetable cultivation was beneficial as it contained in full measure essential elements for good growth. However, since the last 2-3 years, factory waste was being drained into the sewers and this had increased the chemical content of the water. As a result, the following harm was being caused to vegetable crops. In summer, as soon as small plants were watered, the acid contained in the water caused the plants to wither away. For the above reason, the summer vegetable crop was nearly given up. The shine of the vegetable thus cultivated was not healthy. For cultivation in this situation, additional fertilizers and medicines were required. Until last year, Dayaram and Mathura Singh were growing vegetables on seven and 15 acres of land, respectively. But with extensive use of sewer water, vegetables turned red in colour and there were harmful effects. As a result, it became difficult to keep the saplings live in the early stages. The cost of production had increased alongside the diminishing returns. These two persons, therefore, discontinued vegetable farming in this village and migrated to village Prahladpur where there was no such water-related problem.

In village Badoli, the farmers growing vegetables were in a dilemma, as the cost incurred in growing vegetables was not being met by the returns. They were depressed because the sewer water besides harming the crops also required extra cost on fertilizers and medicines. To earn their livelihood, these people have started buying vegetables from the wholesale markets and selling them in the weekly markets, thereby earning Rs. 100-150 on a daily basis.

Village Unchagaon (Gujjar Mohalla) — Interaction with Consumer Groups

A visit to village Unchagaon was undertaken on 25th March, 2003 around 11-00 a.m.

We approached local PCO booth in the Gujjar Mohalla to inquire about the location of the Saini Mohalla. Later, we could see two women making cow dung cakes nearby. We approached them to learn about the consumption of vegetables and what activities they do about their livelihoods. We met Bedbati Devi and Sarla Devi (a widow) who are two sisters and have been married into the same family to two brothers. They have four buffaloes each giving on average eight to ten kilos of milk everyday though in the peak season the quantity can even go up to 12 kilos a day. After their home consumption is met with, the remaining is sold at Rs.14 to Rs.15 a kilo to certain fixed houses on a monthly payment basis. They also sell the cow dung cake. For eight months in a year they make cow dung cakes and stack them while for the four rainy months they collect the cow dung and use it as manure for their own fields on which they cultivate wheat/barsam. The cow dung cakes are sold for Rs. 30 a maund/40 kg. And there are 12 cow dung cakes in five kilos, i.e. 96 to 100 cakes in one maund.

Although the women are illiterate their children attend school. Two of their daughters are in the college of Bedbati and Sarla's son studies in class ten.

They do not cultivate vegetables in their field as it involves hard work and labour. Their children go to school and are not interested in doing the work related to vegetable cultivation. However, some green vegetables such as *turai*, *bottle gourd*, *palak*, *bathua*, etc. are casually grown in their field though not for commercial purposes. These green vegetables are grown on their own on the fields.Vegetables for domestic consumption are generally purchased from the market.

Shri Netram Gujjar, nephew of the two women, joined the discussions at this stage.

Consumption

The consumption pattern of vegetables was discussed. Green seasonal vegetables are consumed by them.The main vegetable consumed was potato as it went well with all sorts of dishes. Vegetables were expensive and it had a direct correlation with the available funds. They consumed cauliflower, *palak* and *bhindi* but only occasionally when they had money to buy or when these vegetables became cheap in the market. Their children also started consuming whatever vegetables are cooked in the house from the early age of one year.

Cauliflower

Cauliflower is consumed mainly to fill the stomach and the women were aware that there is not much of food value from this vegetable and causes flatulence. The cooking pattern was also described. The cauliflower was first cut into florets and washed. The insects, if any, were removed while cutting and washing. The *massala* is fried in oil and then the florets are cooked alongwith the massala. This vegetable is consumed once or twice in a week.

Bhindi

Bhindi is first washed and then cut into pieces. This is cooked with *ajwain*, *haldi*, *masala* and some lemon juice is added after cooking to reduce juice content of bhindi. This vegetable is also consumed once or twice a week. It does not have much vitamins and causes flatulence and pain in the legs.

Spinach

Nutritional value is most in palak. This is a green vegetable and is preferred.The palak leaves are first washed in a lot of water so that the dust settles down. The leaves are then cut into pieces and cooked. Palak juice is prepared and given to the children.

Pregnant mothers are not encouraged to eat either cauliflower or bhindi, as both these vegetables cause flatulence and body aches. These women are given more of dal, milk and rotis.

The two women stated that they generally got advice on vegetable cultivation from the traders of seeds, fertilizers and pesticides. These traders have books on such information which they consult and give advice.

The idea of visiting the Saini Mohalla was dropped as there had been a mishap in the Mohalla and the whole community was likely to be disturbed.

Village Chandawali (Saini Mohalla)—Producer Group

We next proceeded to village Chandawali and met a family group of vegetable cultivators. Smt. Vidya along with her daughter Anita and son Rajkumar were engaged in field work. They were also attending the buffaloes. The mother is illiterate but the children attend school. Anita is in the 8th class and Rajkumar studies in 11th class.

The family has about two bigha of land and grows mainly pudina, palak, dhania, ghiya, petha, turai, karela, cauliflower, bhindi, etc. They sell off most of the vegetables grown. The son carries the vegetables to the market for sale to the whole sellers in Ballabhgarh. Some vegetable cultivators employ daily labour on payment of Rs. 50 per day in peak seasons.

Dhania and pudina are cultivated all round the year and petha, ghiya, turai and karela cultivation starts from the third month of the year. This is done as a form of crop rotation.

They prefer to eat palak. The leaves are first washed in bucket full of water to remove the dust, then cut up, washed and then boiled. Palak may be washed even thrice if there is lot of dust. The boiled palak is then mashed up and cooked with potato. Palak is also cooked with atta to make a filling dish. The juice of the leaves is thrown away and not used.They are aware of the food value of palak and this information has been received by them from the school teacher and doctor.

Children like to eat bhindi although they know that this vegetable causes flatulence.

Besides vegetable cultivation, the family also had milk from the buffaloes. On an average, there was 14-15 kilos of milk from one buffalo during peak season and 2-3 kilos during lean months.

For construction of the canal, the government has taken up the land and the available land for cultivation of vegetables has been reduced. Most families had small pieces of land and many of them had constructed houses on these plots.

As cultivators of vegetables, the group felt that there was a lot of hard work involved. Urea, cow dung and DAP were used in cultivation. The proportion was 50 paisa cow dung and one rupee urea. While urea and cow dung enhanced the growth rate of the plants, DAP gave strength. The gas content of the cow dung gave a fillip to the plant growth. Sometimes, cow dung generates termites and pesticides had to be used. The quantity of pesticide used was decided at random by the group depending on the growth of insects in the crops. Insecticides were sprayed on the crop with great care so that the poisonous effects on humans are avoided. They waited for one hour before going near the fields and washed their hands with clay and soap. With less insects, one or two caps full of the medicine is sprayed and with more insects, sometimes the full bottle is used up. One bottle costs Rs. 50 and is enough for an area less than ½ bigha.

Before the vegetables are taken to the market for sale, they wash these in the kundi adjacent to the fields. The *kundi* is filled up by drawing water through a electric pump. The charges for electricity consumption are 250–300 rupees in every two months. The *kundi* is cleaned 3-4 times a year with cleaning powder. After spraying pesticides in the morning, the vegetables are cut the following day. The vegetables are put in buckets and washed separately so that the pesticides are washed away. After the first washing, these are put inside the kundi and given a final wash.

As they grow vegetables, they do not buy from the market. They have to buy potatoes, oil, clothes and pulses from the market.

3

LIVELIHOOD STRATEGIES AND ROLE OF HORTICULTURE PRODUCERS—VARANASI

The villages in the peri-urban areas of Varanasi have diverse sources of livelihoods. They include the following:

- Cultivation of crops such as paddy/wheat,
- Cultivation of vegetables,
- *Saree* weaving,
- Making bead necklaces/bangles,
- *Bindi* pasting,
- Shopkeeping,
- *Bidi* rolling,
- Daily labour,
- Government service,
- Private employment, and
- Business.

Women, men and children are all involved in activities related to farming including horticulture cultivation, *saree* weaving, daily labour and other activities. There is division of labour in selected activities such as saree weaving where men do the weaving while women help in rolling the thread. However, women are generally engaged in rolling of *bidi* and pasting of *bindi*. In vegetable cultivation, women, men and children participate in different activities from sowing to marketing. In some villages, cultivation of crops and vegetables is the primary source of livelihoods, while in other villages, saree weaving is considered as a major source of business. In some villages, there is also the trend of selling cultivable land and adopting other sources of livelihoods such as saree weaving. Some men are withdrawing from cultivation of crops and vegetables and getting engaged in saree weaving and other activities.

In the peri-urban areas of Varanasi, horticulture is practised, especially vegetable cultivation, which is an important source of livelihood. With small sized land holdings vegetable cultivation is looked upon as a lucrative avenue of income. Some of the vegetables cultivated in the peri-urban areas of Varanasi are as follows:

- Okra
- Cauliflower
- Spinach
- Tomato
- Potato
- Lufafa
- Bitter gourd
- Bottle gourd
- Cucumber
- Green peas
- Turai
- Bora
- Others

Table 3.1 provides an idea of vegetable cultivation in the peri-urban areas of Varanasi. Not all localities grow all the vegetables mentioned above. In some areas the main vegetable grown is okra in three cycles, while in other areas spinach is grown in three cycles and in still other areas it is cauliflower grown in five or six cycles. Hence, there are wide variations in patterns of horticulture cultivation in the peri-urban Varanasi in terms of proportion, acreage, productivity and the number of households growing them. It is evident that the peri-urban areas of Varanasi have specialised in producing different vegetables and they have diverse perspectives and preferences in cultivating them. As we shall see later that in terms of food safety the production practices are not that safe and the quality of vegetables get compromised to that extent.

In the peri-urban areas of Varanasi, the land is suitable for cultivation of vegetables. Peri-urban villages around Varanasi supply a good proportion of vegetables to the Varanasi market from where they are transported to many other cities in addition to meeting local demands of consumers in Varanasi. In some peri-urban villages most household land is utilised for cultivation of vegetables.

Who Does What?

- All members of family work together to prepare the field for sowing and for irrigating it.
- The men buy seeds.

Table 3.1: Varanasi—Vegetable Cultivation and Livelihoods—An Overview

Peri-Urban Hamlet/ village in Varanasi	*Significance of vegetable cultivation as source of livelihood*	*No. of households growing vegetables and doing other activities*	*Area under vegetable cultivation as proportion of total cultivable area*
1. Rajbhar Hamlet, Parampur Village	Medium	Total of 130 households - Vegetable cultivation (130 HH) - Daily labour (30 HH) - Saree weaving (20 HH)	Total cultivable land: 145 acres Okra – 28 per cent Spinach – 1.4 per cent
2. Bangla Tola, Parampur Village	High	Total of 58 households - Vegetable cultivation (58 HH) - Daily wage-earner (18 HH) - Saree weaving (30 HH)	Total cultivable land: 31 acres Okra – 42 per cent Spinach –23 per cent Cauliflower – 0.5 per cent
3. Morya Hamlet, Lohta Village	Low	Total of 83 households - Vegetable cultivation (83 HH) - General cultivation (83 HH) - Saree weaving (25 HH) - Daily wage (10 HH)	Total cultivable land: 35 acres Cauliflower – 0.2 per cent Spinach – 4 per cent
4. Morya Hamlet, Bharthara Village	High	Total of 53 households - Vegetable cultivation (53 HH) - General cultivation (53 HH) - Daily labour (13 HH)	Total cultivable land: 81 acres Cauliflower – 53.09 per cent Spinach – 4.9 per cent Okra –1.2 per cent
5. Pal Hamlet, Bharthara Village	Medium	Total of 64 households - Vegetable cultivation (64 HH) - General cultivation (64 HH) - Daily labour (20 HH)	Total cultivable land: 55 acres Cauliflower – 18.2 per cent Spinach – 18.2 per cent Okra – 3.6 per cent
6. Patel Hamlet, Maraw Village	Medium	Total of 80 Households - Vegetable cultivation (80 HH) - General cultivation (80 HH) - Daily labour (50 HH)	Total cultivable land: 165 acres Cauliflower – 37 per cent Okra – 0.6 per cent Spinach – 2.4 per cent
7. Morya Hamlet, Maraw Village	Medium	Total of 26 Households - Vegetable cultivation (26 HH) - General cultivation (26 HH) - Saree weaving (26 HH)	Total cultivable land: 57 acres Cauliflower – 32.3 per cent Okra – 3.2 per cent Spinach – 8.1 per cent

Note: Significance of vegetable cultivation as a source of livelihood is "high" if the proportion of cultivable land growing vegetables (okra + spinach + cauliflower) is more than 50 per cent. It is "medium" if such proportion is below 50 per cent but above 30 per cent. It is "low" if it is below 30 per cent.

- The women and children do the weeding.
- The men apply the fertilizers and pesticides.
- Women, men and children do harvesting and prepare bundles of vegetables.
- The men take the vegetables to the market and sell them.

Some households, which are economically better off and have access to agricultural land, cultivate vegetables and crops mostly for commercial purposes. Such households can manage water from their own pump sets or make payment to their neighbours. Some households with marginal land holdings grow vegetables in small quantities for self-consumption. Of the three vegetables under consideration in this study – cauliflower, okra and spinach – the pattern and proportions of vegetable cultivation vary across villages as shown in Table 3.1. Whereas in some hamlets such as Rajbhar (village Parampur), okra is cultivated extensively in other hamlets such as Morya (village Lohta), spinach is preferred while in Maraw, it is production of cauliflower. Some households possessing marginal land holdings and homestead garden cultivate vegetables mainly for personal consumption. A few of them sell vegetables only if they are in excess of what they need to consume.

Cauliflower is consumed in the famous festival of the villagers—Khichri (Makar Sankranti). The villagers celebrate this festival with fresh rice from their fields and cauliflower-potato-peas-tomato mixed vegetable and sweet (Dhundha) prepared with jaggery (extracted from sugarcane cultivated on their own land).

3.1 SEASONALITY OF VEGETABLE CULTIVATION

Many vegetables are cultivated in summer, rainy and winter seasons:

- The main summer and rainy vegetables are okra, turai and bora.
- During winter, tomato, peas, radish and cauliflower are cultivated.

There are three cycles of okra cultivated locally referred to as Maghi, Baisakhi and Barsati. The cultivation of Baisakhi okra starts from Baisakh after the wheat is harvested. The production starts from mid-Jeth and continues till Kartik/mid Aghan. The cultivation of Barsati okra starts from Asar while the production starts from mid-Sraban and continues until Kartik/Aghan. The cultivation of Maghi okra starts from Magh while the production starts from mid-Chet and continues till Baisakh-mid Jeth:

- Turai-cultivation starts from Jeth and continues until Kartik.
- Spinach is cultivated in Baisakh, Jeth, Asar, Kuwar and Phagun.
- Cauliflower is cultivated in Aghan, Poosh and Magh.
- Lufafa is cultivated in Magh, Phagun and Chet.
- Tomato and green peas cultivation starts from Kartik and continues until Poosh.
- Bora cultivation starts from Jeth and continues until Kartik.
- Wheat cultivation starts from Aghan and gets harvested in Baisakh. After harvesting okra is cultivated.
- Paddy cultivation starts in Jeth and harvesting is done in Kartik/ Agahan.
- Sugarcane—A relatively small proportion of land engaged for sugarcane cultivation remains throughout the year.
- Okra in Baisakh, Ashar and Magh.

3.2 WHY VEGETABLES ARE CULTIVATED?

Vegetables are cultivated for different reasons as explained by the horticulture producers in the peri-urban areas of Varanasi, some of which are listed below:

- For having income through selling them — they get almost equal income through spinach and cauliflower.
- For home consumption — they eat mostly spinach and cauliflower.
- For good health — they consider spinach as highly nutritious.
- For higher productivity — spinach and okra have high production.
- For maintaining horticulture as an alternate source of livelihood.
- For better utilization of cultivable land.
- To grow suitable vegetables which are compatible with the soil.
- To boost main or supplementary sources of income.
- To have opportunities of quick income.
- To utilize relatively smaller sized land resulting from sub-division and fragmentation of land.

3.3 TRENDS IN HORTICULTURE PRODUCTION AND PRACTICES

In some study villages, farmers are cultivating vegetables since 1945 when lufafa, bitter gourd, potato and onion were produced in small quantities occupying less than 10 per cent of cultivable land. Gradually, the proportion of vegetable cultivation increased and okra cultivation started in 1965. In 1970s, fertilizers and pesticides started getting applied to vegetable cultivation and its area increased as much as 75 per cent of total cultivable land. Since 1980, cultivation of cauliflower has almost stopped in some villages due to high cost of production and high incidence of pests. In some other villages, vegetable cultivation started around 1960 when vegetables such as makoi, bitter gourd and pumpkin were grown.

In many villages, okra was cultivated since 1960 when okra seeds were scattered on the land and then ploughed with a wooden plough and bullocks. Such cultivation did not require irrigation, fertilizers and pesticide. There was a ready wholesale market available in Varanasi, named Sanua chatti. Since 1990, okra farming was more organized with chemical inputs and since 1995 okra was planted on rows of earthen mounds, which yielded better results. Of late, there is some fall in cultivation of okra due to problems in harvesting. The people who harvest okra can easily fall sick due to red patches and itching all over the body caused by insects found on okra plants. So one can discern a tendency to move from cultivation of okra to spinach.

3.4 HISTORICAL AGRO-TRANSECT OF OKRA

A historical agro-transect of okra, constructed on the basis of oral history by women groups interacted in the peri-urban areas of Varanasi, provides a background of how cultivation of okra shaped up over the past years. See box 5.

Okra is not a new vegetable cultivated by the villagers. It has been cropped since long years though its variety has undergone change from local to hybrid. Spinach also has a long history as illustrated in box 6.

Box 5: Historical Agro-transect of Okra in Rajbhar, Parampur, Varanasi

In the 1960s, around 40 years back, there was no water facility. The vegetables were grown only in rainy season.The vegetables grown were—okra, khira, turai, tinda, arui, etc. The land was left fallow for some period where livestock was kept for a few days. Their droppings were used as manure for the fields. There were no insects and no insecticides used. The villagers applied ashes on plants.

Around 1966, there was a massive change in crop area with availability of water facility. The villagers started experimenting with small amounts of fertiliser and insecticides, which had considerable impact on production thus enhancing farmers' confidence. Vegetable cultivation started in winter and summer seasons on a commercial basis. In 1980s, a variety of okra was introduced by the name of "Satdharia", which had seven divisions on the surface of the vegetable. The plants sprouted many stems. The yield increased remarkably leading to high profits. Farmers kept applying more fertilisers and for counteracting insects they applied higher dose of insecticides.

"Satdharia" variety could not be sustained over a long period and a better looking variety was planted by the name of "Pachdharia". This type of okra is sleek and long. The plants do not sprout many stems similar to "Satdharia". This variety has been grown extensively. The local variety of okra is susceptible to *Kabrawaha* disease.

(*Contd.*)

(*Contd.*)

Doses of fertilizer and insecticide have increased over time. In 1995-96, a hybrid variety of okra was introduced. Now the farmers are cultivating its seed. The women rate it as a preferred variety because of the following merits:

- The incidence of "*Kabrawaha*" disease found in okra is marginal and chances of other diseases are less.
- This variety of okra can be cultivated during summer as well as during rainy season.
- The return is high.
- It starts yielding fruit after one and half months.
- The stems can be cut for next crop (kalam).

At present cultivation of okra and other crops is falling because the younger generation does not prefer to be cultivators and the land per head is also declining with increase in population and fragmentation of land. Most people now prefer the Ashari okra in the rainy season, which can grow with the help of rainwater.

Source: Based on interaction with women group, Rajbhar hamlet, Parampur, Varanasi, Facilitator — Meera Jayaswal.

Box 6: Historical Agro-transect of Spinach in Morya, Lohta, Varanasi

In 1942, the local people grew maize, makoi, kakri, spinach in small quantity with manure neem and sold it to Chanua mandi in Varanasi. In 1950, spinach cultivation increased in quantity and some tomato and cauliflower were also planted. Chemical fertilizers started to be used while the seed was of local variety. In 1960, spinach cultivation underwent further increase together with tomato and cauliflower with the help of local variety seeds. In 1970, there was further increase in cultivation of spinach and brinjal growing was also tried for commercial purposes with the help of local variety seeds. Bicycle was the main source of carrying goods to the market. In 1980, market demand led to large increase in spinach cultivation with hybrid seeds and chemical fertilizers. Vegetables were transported to markets in Varanasi with the help of bus and bicycles. In 1990, spinach cultivation increased further and also in neighbouring villages with the help of hybrid seeds, chemical fertilizers and pesticides.

Source: Men group, Morya Hamlet, Lohta Village, Varanasi.

3.5 PREFERENCES FOR VEGETABLE CULTIVATION

Preferences for vegetable cultivation vary in the peri-urban areas of Varanasi. Though cauliflower gives the highest income, cultivation of spinach yields quick money. Cauliflower needs high levels of irrigation and its yield is high though the impact of insects on cauliflower is the highest. Spinach bears the brunt of weather but yields quick production.

3.6 PREFERENCE FOR OKRA

In few villages with adequate water facility, both women and men prefer to grow okra. As per the views expressed by men group/s from the peri-urban Varanasi, their preference for cultivating okra is for the following reasons:

- There is relatively high yield from okra cultivation and the fertility of the soil is good,
- All members of the household can remain involved in such cultivation,
- There is marketing facility available and the okra crop can be harvested quickly,
- The impact of weather on the crop is negligible, and
- The okra plants can be later dried and used as fuel for cooking.

Many women living in the peri-urban areas of Varanasi have detailed knowledge about ways of cultivating vegetables. They have been involved in such cultivation since their childhood. Asha, a women participant, remarked with confidence, "We were cultivating cauliflower and spinach as children before getting married and coming to this village". In terms of cultivation, the women preferred okra (first), spinach (second) and cauliflower (third). The women groups' preference for okra is based on the advantages as shown in Table 3.2.

Table 3.2: Okra Cultivation: Perceived Advantages, Problems and Constraints

Advantages	*Problems/Constraints*
More income	More insects
Yielding daily income	Require more insecticide
Continuity in earnings for six months	Need more fertilisers
Less labour intensive	
Quick harvesting	
Less damage during adverse weather	
High yielding	
Easy market facility and high demand	
Local soil compatibility	
Availability of water	

Note: Women participants, Rajbhar hamlet, Parampur, Varanasi.

More Income

Okra cultivation generates more income as compared to spinach and cauliflower or any other vegetables, which are being grown in the hamlet. Okra has high return due to long and continuous yield of eight months. Taken together, all the three varieties of okra start producing yield from mid-Chet and continue until mid-Aghan. The harvest is huge with at least two-three harvesting done weekly. Moreover, the income multiplies because it is a major vegetable in summer and in the rainy season. The bottle-gourd is also available in the summer season but it is not preferred for consumption by all local people. Parval and other vegetables are imported from places outside Varanasi and are quite expensive. From mid-Asar, Bora harvesting starts.,Turai harvesting starts from Sraban, after the price of okra comes down. Okra as a vegetable serves the summer and the rainy seasons, when there is dearth in availability of other popular vegetables. Okra's demand is very high in the local market and yields relatively higher income than other vegetables.

Yields Daily Income

Due to the advantage of intermittent harvesting, daily income is high in okra as compared to any other crop. It takes care of the daily household expenses of the villagers and there is no need to search opportunities for daily labour for those cultivating okra, especially in the summer season when heat is almost unbearable.

Continuity in Earnings for Six Months

Okra yields income over a stretch of eight months, which compares favourably with many other crops in terms of income, which is generated in the process. Each third/fourth day it is harvested and in a month the total harvest is around twelve to fifteen times.

Less Labour Intensive

Okra is preferred because it is less labour intensive than cauliflower. Kalawati, a women participant, remarked that okra is less labour intensive, especially in summer when there is less grass and weeding of grass once a month is enough. There is also not much need to remove insects from okra plants as compared to cauliflower plants where insect removal is a regular job for women.

Quick Harvesting

The interval between the cultivation and yield of okra is about one and a half-month. Thus the interval is very short. The cultivators don't have to wait for much time for yield as in the case of potato and cauliflower.

Less Damage During Adverse Weather

The probability of damage is less in okra. The adverse weather, rain cloud and fog do not damage okra as they do to spinach and cauliflower.

High Yielding

The yield of okra is high. It can be harvested every third day during rainy season (one-day interval) and on every fourth day during summer season (two-days interval).

Easy Market Facility and High Demand

There exists good market facility for okra in the city of Varanasi. In the market the demand is quite high because the suppliers come to Varanasi for procuring vegetables. Traders come from far away places such as Mughalsarai, Jaunpur, Allahabad, etc. The supply does not exceed demand and the price realised is lucrative because a small belt of Varanasi is engaged in okra cultivation, mostly due to availability of water facility and soil compatibility.

Local Soil Compatible With Okra

There are few pockets in the Varanasi district, where okra is grown extensively. Most areas of agricultural land do not have irrigation facility during the summer season. Moreover, soil is not compatible to suit okra cultivation. In addition, the small landholders cannot afford to cultivate okra for commercial purposes for its long duration. Their crop preferences and means do not suit okra cultivation.

Availability of Water

During the summer season, there is need for sufficient water for okra. In villages such as Parampur, the farmers are fortunate to have a government boring water facility. There is no dearth of water.

Although much of the agricultural land is up-land, which is suitable for vegetable cultivation selected obstacles stand in the way of not cultivating horticulture produce such as okra.

Problems in Growing Okra

While discussing the advantages of growing okra, the women also indicated the problems associated with okra cultivation. One problem is of higher incidence of insect in okra as compared to other vegetables though less than that of cauliflower. In order to prevent damage by insects, high level of insecticides needs to be applied to okra, on a weekly or bi-weekly basis depending on the infestation. As okra is harvested frequently, more fertilizer is required on a weekly basis to rejuvenate the soil. Despite the obstacles to okra cultivation, its advantages clearly outweigh its problems.

3.7 ECONOMICS OF HORTICULTURE PRODUCTION

Amongst the three vegetables under reference in this study, okra is an important commercial vegetable. As for the costs, output and income on vegetables the following table is illustrative. Cultivation of okra is considered relatively profitable as compared to spinach though its input cost is also higher. The local participants also explained that they were able to plant other vegetables on the same field as okra (e.g. cucumber, bitter gourd and lufafa), which was not possible in case of spinach. The weather has minor or no impact on okra crop as compared to spinach. The harvest from okra can continue throughout the year by planting two sets of crops, while the crop available from spinach was for a shorter period.

There are three crops of okra cultivated in the peri-urban areas of Varanasi. Okra crops planted thrice a year yield harvest throughout the year. As and when the okra harvest declines, the plants are treated with another round of fertilizers and pesticides after removing their shoots and dry branches. When the okra plants stop harvesting, some farmers let the plants dry and use them for supporting vegetable plants such as lufafa, which are creepers. For low lying land in the village, the farmers grow paddy when they are waterlogged. But soon after harvesting paddy, the farmers grow okra on the same land. There are three cycles of okra grown in the peri-urban areas of Varanasi:

- Maghi — sown in Magh — can be harvested until Jeth,
- Chaiti — sown in Chet — can be harvested until Kuwar, and
- Barsati — sown in Asar — can be harvested until Aghan.

For cauliflower, seeds are planted in the month of Jeth and the harvest is used mostly for home consumption. For spinach, the sowing starts in the month of Ashar and two crops are harvested from Sraban onwards until Kartik. Spinach is grown in small quantities mostly for home consumption.

The cost of vegetable cultivation varies across the type of vegetable cultivated, the season for cultivation, the size of land, the inputs used. The main inputs are as follows:

- Land preparation costs,
- Seed,
- Fertilizer,
- Insecticide,
- Irrigation,

- Marketing/transportation cost, and
- Hiring of labour, if any, for weeding, harvesting, etc.

Many peri-urban hamlets in Varanasi have government and private tube-well and pump sets and also have *pucca* irrigation channels running across their fields. The farmers use hybrid seeds and chemical fertilisers and pesticides for the crops grown. Okra and spinach require less fertilisers. Pesticides are required in high doses for cauliflower, followed by okra and less for spinach.

Table 3.3: Yield, Inputs and Returns of Cauliflower Varieties

Criteria Yield (flowers)	*Kauri 600*	*Kartiki 500*	*Aghani 400 very large flowers*	*Pusi 400 very large flowers*	*Maghi 400*	*Sonobal 600*
Expenditure	680	650	580	220	450	690
Rate	8	8	6	6	6	6
Return	4800	4000	2400	2400	2400	3600
Net return	4120	3350	1820	2180	1950	2910
Time	6	5	4	4	4	4
Monthly return	686.67	670.00	455.00	545.00	487.50	727.50
Inputs in cauliflower in one Bisa (Rs.)						
Jotai	20	20	20	20	20	20
Bhari	30	20	20	20	10	20
Bijai	10	10	10	10	250	300
Fertilizers	250	250	250	100	100	200
Chirkai	300	300	250	50	50	100
Nirai/gurai	70	50	30	20	20	50
Total	650	650	580	220	450	690

Participants: Kalavati, Hiravati, Urmila, Sita; dated 17-10-01; Place: Morya Hamlet, Village Bharthara; Facilitator: Meera Jayaswal.

Table 3.3 shows yield, inputs and returns from six varieties of cauliflower, Kauri, Katki, Aghani, Pusi, Maghi and Sonobal named on the basis of their harvesting months. Table 3.3 gives the yields, inputs and returns from the different varieties of cauliflower. In terms of costs, Pusi is the cheapest followed by Maghi, though Sonobal provides the highest monthly return.

The reasons for cultivating palak were explored by the women of village Bharthara through the method of *criteria scoring* and the results are given in Table 3.4. The table shows that on at least criteria—income flow, knowledge of cultivation, labour required and income, spinach scored the highest.

Table 3.4: Criteria Scoring for Palak Cultivation, for Hamlet Morya, Village Bharthara (10 = high; 1 = low)

Criteria	*Score*
Income flows are regular	10
Knowledge about its cultivation	10
Less labour is required	10
Women get an opportunity to work in vegetable cultivation	6
Higher income	10
Consumption	6

Participants: Israuti, Sita, Pushpa, Laxmi, Prabhavati; dated 22-10-01; Place: Morya Hamlet, Village Bharthara; Facilitator: Meera Jayaswal.

The average yield, inputs and returns from the cultivation of spinach in village Bharthara are given in Table 3.5, which shows the variation in returns and net income.

Table 3.5: Average Yield, Inputs and Returns from Palak Cultivation

Criteria	*Bhado*	*Kuar*	*Kartik*	*Aghan*	*Poosh*
Yield	Cultivated	100 kg	150 kg	100 kg	100 kg
Rate	—	8-10	5-6	4-5	4-5
Return	—	800-1000	750-900	400-500	400-500
Expenditure	100	50	50	50	50
Net income	-100	750-950	700-850	350-450	350-450

Participants: Kalavati, Hiravati, Urmila, Sita; dated 17-10-01; Place: Morya Hamlet, Village Bharthara; Facilitator: Meera Jayaswal.

Okra is not cultivated in the Hamlet on a large scale because there is not enough land to spare since this vegetable engages the land for a longer time and the soil is unsuitable.

A set of expenditure and income for cultivation of three cycles of okra in Rajbhar hamlet, Parampur village and four cycles of spinach in Morya hamlet, Lohta village is given in Tables 3.6. It can be observed from Table 3.6 that the average net income from the three cycles of okra per bisa comes to Rs. 1,550 (Maghi), Rs. 2,955 (Baisakhi) and Rs. 2,610 (Barsati). The monthly income comes to Rs. 310, Rs. 422 and Rs. 435 respectively, which is higher for Barsati okra.

Table 3.6: Expenditure/Income from Vegetables (Unit: in Rs. Per bisa or 0.03 acre)

Input/ Output/ Income	*E/I Okra-Chaiti/ Baisakhi*	*E/I Okra-Maghi*	*E/I Okra-Barsati*	*E/I Spinach-Kunwar*	*E/I Spinach-Sraban*	*E/I Spinach-Aghan*	*E/I Spinach-Poosh*
Input cost	1,395	1,010	790	153	160	180	135
Total income	4,350	2,560	3,400	400	750	1,200	1,000
Net income	2,955	1,550	2,610	247	590	1,020	865
Net income per month	422	310	435				

Notes: Estimates provided by village participants—women group, Village-Rajbhar hamlet, Parampur (for Okra estimates), men group, Morya hamlet, Lohta (Spinach estimates); Facilitator—Meera Jayaswal.

3.8 LOCAL PERSPECTIVES ON NUTRITION IN HORTICULTURE

The men and the women groups in the peri-urban areas of Varanasi have their gendered views on nutrition in horticulture as indicated in Table 3.7.

Both women and men groups in different hamlets of peri-urban Varanasi did not perceive okra as nutritious, yet they preferred to cultivate it. The nutritional value of the selected horticulture produce did not affect their choice of vegetable cultivation. The cultivation pattern of vegetables was determined more by the price in the market, the size of land holding and the socio-economic status of the households rather than by their perceived nutritional content.

3.9 PRE- AND POST-HANDLING OF HORTICULTURE PRODUCE

In the Rajbhar hamlet, the marketing of vegetables involves the following steps:

- *Harvesting okra*—All family members — men, women and children are involved.
- *Sorting into various types*—Okra is sorted in four qualities—high quality (tender and soft), medium quality (slight stiff), low quality (deformed) and throwaway type (excess insects). High and medium qualities of okra are sent to the market, the low quality is kept for personal use and the worst is given to the livestock. All family members—men, women and children are involved in sorting vegetables.

Table 3.7: Gendered Perspectives on Nutrition in Vegetables

Hamlet/Village	*Women Group's Perspective on Nutrition*	*Men Group's Perspective on Nutrition*
Rajbhar Hamlet	Women rated spinach as most nutritious in comparison to cauliflower and okra.	They liked the taste of lufafa to okra, and its medicinal property of providing strength. On the nutritional values of okra, spinach and cauliflower, the men group compared them on the basis of different criteria and concluded that spinach has the maximum nutrition, followed by cauliflower and okra.
Bangla Tola	The women mentioned that spinach was the most nutritious vegetable grown locally and cauliflower was more nutritious than okra.	The men perceived spinach to be much more nutritious than okra though for gastric problems okra was more beneficial than spinach. They thought that the seeds inside okra helped in keeping the stomach clean.
Morya Hamlet, Village Lohta	The women thought that spinach was a nutritious vegetable.	The men liked the taste of gobhi, had less preference for spinach, lufafa and okra. They thought that cauliflower had the least nutrition and spinach had the highest nutritional value. It was good for vitamin, energy, blood formation, eye sight and for preventing gastric disease. Juice made of spinach was highly beneficial for gastric disease.
Morya Hamlet, Village Bharthara	The women did not mention any strength of cauliflower. They were not aware of the various nutrients like proteins, calcium, carotene, iron, etc. They had no notion of the strength giving vegetables, those causing flatulence etc. Spinach, tomato and carrot were perceived as most nutritive and potato and cauliflower, the least.	The men group regarded spinach as very nutritional, found cabbage had no taste and gave an odour They were aware of the nutritive value of spinach. They thought spinach juice was beneficial for gastric related disorders. They recognized the nutritive value of cabbage, but disliked its taste. They did not have any idea of the nutritive value of cauliflower and potato.

Note: Collated from field notes on Varanasi.

- *Transportation to the market*—Usually young/adult male member of an HH goes to the market on bicycle. If the vegetables are in large quantities, he goes by bus. As for women-headed households, the women go to the wholesale market by bus but find it difficult to load and unload vegetables as illustrated in Box 7.

Box 7: Story of Asha, a Women-headed Household from Rajbhar Hamlet, Parampur

Asha, aged 35 years, is widow. She has 10 bisa of land for vegetable growing. She has not been allowed to remain in her house. Currently living in a Marai. It is a one clay room, which is a temporary room, with straw on the roof. There is no window, only space but no door. She gets up around 4 a.m. in the morning, cooks by 6 a.m. Immediately goes to the field with sons and harvests vegetables, screens them and goes to the Chanua market alone. If her son accompanies her then it is expensive because she will have to pay the bus fare. Though reaching *Arhatia* is not difficult, it is difficult to load and unload. She has developed stomachache.

- As soon as the horticulture produce is brought to the market, the *Arhatia* (middleman) assesses and finds out a good buyer. As there is commission, there is no difficulty for the middleman to find out a suitable buyer.
- In a market dominated by men, the women find marketing of vegetables difficult.
- Local transportation is difficult. The women are required to carry the produce by bus to nearby wholesale market.
- The women in some villages are of the opinion that if male members can form a group for transporting produce to distant market, the profits realized can be high.
- The women are looking for information on different markets so that they can procure the best price. The present marketing system does not facilitate the local people to get good price. The wholesale prices received by the producers are generally very low.

As regards the issue of pre-and post-handling of horticulture produce, the participants in the peri-urban villages described various related activities such as the involvement of various household members, exposure to contamination, which impacts on safety of horticulture produce, the awareness level, management skills of the producers, etc. See Table 3.8.

The exposure of vegetables to contamination was from different sources as listed below:

- Soil
- Water
- Fertilizer
- Pesticide
- Dust
- Wild animals, pet dogs and livestock

Table 3.8: Pre- and Post-harvest Handling of the Vegetables

Pre-post harvesting stages/activities	*The exposure to contamination*	*The awareness level of women*
Soil	Too much fertilizer, dogs roaming around, human defecation.	The soil absorbs all dirt. There is no effect on plants.
Water	Irrigation sources, washing procedure.	The drains/gutters are in very bad condition, leading to contaminated water.
Dust	The plants, vegetables	The dust does no harm. After wash, it goes away. There is no impact of dust.
Vehicular pollution	The cultivation is exposed to vehicular pollution	The emissions of the vehicles do not cause any harm to the plants including vegetables.
Brick kiln	A few brick kilns are near the village	The emissions of the brick kilns do not cause any harm to the plants including vegetables, which are adjacent. The smoke harms vegetables grown at a distance of 1/2 km.
Fertilizer	Use is increasing. Manure is not applied rather used as fuel for cooking.	Women think that the excessive use of fertilizer does not contaminate soil. It decreases the strength, but there is no alternative, If fertilizers are not applied, there will be no yield, and they will die of starvation. Women made clear that there is cow dung, which can be applied, but then that will create the problem of fuel. The villagers dry and use cow dung as fuel.
Pesticides	The use is increasing very rapidly.	Women think that the excessive use of pesticides contaminates produce. However, there is no significant effect after 6-8 hours.
Pet-dogs	Dogs roam in the cultivated area.	Women believe that the dogs or live stock's droppings do not harm the standing crops, rather it provides nutrition.
Human defecation	There is no latrine/urinating place. The villagers use their cultivated land/other land for defecation	No contamination to the yield is perceived.
Harvesting	The Okra, cauliflower or spinach is not cut after proper hand wash.	No contamination or cross contamination is possible.

Notes: Village participants—Pyari, Kalawati, Saraswati, Asha. *Dated*: 12-10-2001, Village-Rajbhar hamlet, Parampur village; Facilitator: Meera Jayaswal.

- Harvesting and sorting
- Defecation
- Container

The summary of discussion is presented in Table 3.8. It shows how women are not aware of the various exposure of vegetable cultivation to contamination.

3.10 PRESERVATION OF VEGETABLES

Some preservation practices of vegetable produce are as follows:

- Before harvesting, the cauliflower is preserved through sprinkling water and spraying medicine. The bad ones are sold at lower price and some are also used as fodder for livestock.
- Spinach, if not harvested in time, goes bad with leaves turning yellow. Some of it can be sold at lower price while rest is used as fodder for livestock.
- After spraying of medicine, if okra is not harvested in time then they are left to rot in the field, which are cooked by poor households as food.
- In general, the producers harvest the vegetables at appropriate time.
- Weeding is done from time to time.
- The leaves and fruits of plants, which go bad, are removed and thrown away from the field.
- It is believed that use of garlic in excess quantity helps in removing poison from vegetables.

3.11 VEGETABLES MARKETED AND/OR HOME CONSUMED

Over 95 per cent of okra produced is sold in the market and less than five per cent is retained for self-consumption. Generally, vegetable producers in peri-urban Varanasi do not have the practice of exchanging vegetables; rather they gift them to near and dear ones. Inter- or intra-village transactions in vegetables are also not prevalent in the village. Vegetables are locally grown round the year and are mostly sold to whole-sellers or alternatively to the retailers. Households generally consume other vegetables, if available from their own land. Neither large nor small cultivators have the habit of consuming more vegetables. During the summer months of Baisakh and Jeth, the consumption of one's own produce of okra is slightly higher because other vegetables are not available in the field.

In addition, as pointed out by women, their preference for own consumption of okra is on the lower side. It is a dry vegetable and does not go well with *chappati* since it cannot be cooked with gravy or with other vegetables. If it is cooked in the morning for breakfast then other supplements are also needed. This leads to higher expenditure on food.

3.12 TREATING VEGETABLES WITH CHEMICALS

In hamlet Bangla Tola, they utilise around five per cent of the vegetables for home consumption. They do not engage in barter and also do not pay in real terms through vegetables to the daily labourers engaged in their fields. They generally mix a chemical called hypolin on okra to retain its green colour, which has high demand, and fetches good price. Some of them who produce less quantity of vegetables take them to the retailers in different markets in Varanasi at a distance of 1 to 3 km though this means getting lower price than the wholesalers and often selling it to more than one retailer. The buyers prefer green and fresh vegetables; for example, they prefer green and fresh spinach with broad leaves. In keeping with their preferences the producers treat the vegetables with chemicals to get better price.

3.13 PROCESS OF TAKING VEGETABLES TO THE MARKET

Some steps in taking vegetables to the market are listed below:

- Nearly all members of a producer household assemble together to harvest vegetables from their field,
- All members of a household become equally busy in arranging harvested vegetables in basket/s as per their size,
- The men then carry the vegetables to the market either in bus or cycle, and
- The womenfolk carry the surplus vegetables left behind from door to door in order to sell them.

Some steps are taken to increase market value of the vegetables are listed below:

- Four days before harvesting, medicines are sprayed on the vegetables so as to make them look fresh and green,
- Hypolin is sprayed four days before okra is harvested so that it looks green and crisp and becomes free of insects, if any. After harvesting is completed, the bad okra is separated from the good ones and arranged and placed into basket/s.
- In case of cauliflower, medicine is sprayed four days in advance,

which help the pests to perish. After the cauliflower is harvested, the insect-ridden leaves are removed from the cauliflower and they are arranged according to their size.

- Even spinach is sprayed with medicines such as Colenel-8, Roger and Multiplech so the insects perish and its leaves look green and fresh.
- Before sending the spinach to the market, they are harvested and laid on earthen floor and covered with wet jute bag/s and also made into bundles of 250 gm and 500 gm. They are sprayed with water from time to time before being taken to the market.

3.14 MARKETING OF HORTICULTURE PRODUCE

Usually, the vegetables produced in the peri-urban areas of Varanasi are marketed in the city of Varanasi in different markets depending on the distance of the village from the market. There are purchasers coming from Allahabad, Kanpur, Mugalsarai and other places. Since such marketing facilities are available, the vegetable producers take their produce such as okra, cauliflower, spinach, lufafa, etc. to Varanasi. They either use their bicycles or take them on a public bus to the market.

Vegetables produced are sold either in the wholesale market, retail market or to vendors, who go to different localities for selling vegetables. Some women also sell their own vegetables from door to door. The horticulture producers sell 90 to 99 per cent of what they produce and generally retain 1 to 10 per cent for home consumption. They do not sell in the local retail market of the village. They generally prefer selling the produce to the wholesalers. Income is higher when sold to retailer than wholesaler however time taken is much more. It is also convenient for the horticulture producer to get the money from the wholesaler at one go. The vendor who buys directly from the field also pays better price. Vendors most often purchase vegetables directly from the producers' field.

The selling price of vegetables varies across seasons. The following gives an idea of the price variation of spinach depending on the quantity available in the market, the higher the quantity the lower is the price.

Price of spinach
Baisakh and Jeth — Rs. 1.60 per kg
Ashar, Sawan and Bhado — Rs. 6.00 per kg
Kartick to Chet — Re. 1.00 per kg

Box 8: Distance of Markets

The producers of vegetables in Rajbhar hamlet have the choice to take the produce to the following markets:

— Chanua-Distance —(15+15 kms to and fro) — daily
— Gangapur *bazaar* (3+3 kms to and fro) — daily
— Raja talab *bazaar* (2+2 kms to and fro) — Wednesday and Saturday
— Akelwa Chauraha (1+1 kms to and fro).

Their choice is dependent on the season, market price, distance from the market, type of transport, quantum of produce, freshness of the produce, work at hand and cash at hand.

In a discussion on marketing aspects, the following points came to light:

- The villagers carry vegetables to the market on an *ad hoc* basis without any planned strategy to realise immediate and profitable returns from the sale of vegetables.
- The vegetable producers realize that the price paid to them is less than what they should get.
- The traders as procurers of their vegetables are in an advantageous position and they can pay them low price.
- Individually, the vegetable producers hardly have any clout. They do not have any cooperative, neither they are planning to form one.
- The traders buy from them in bulk at a price dictated by them. The traders earn high profits.

Middlemen

- The vegetables are sold in the wholesale market — Chanua, through *Arahatia* (middleman).
- The *Arahatia* deducts 6 to 10 per cent of the commission and one to two kgs of the vegetables.
- He is the mediator between the cultivator (owner) and the traders who are from Allahabad, Kolkata, Kanpur, Mugalsarai, etc.

3.15 INSTITUTIONAL SUPPORT TO HORTICULTURE

The institutional support to horticulture producers is weak and does not function properly as shown in Table 3.9 for three villages. The trader in farm inputs is the most important agent for disseminating information though the person is very much working under profit motive and is not trained to disseminate the right type of information. In absence of any other channel, the producers depend on him for 80 per cent information related to seeds, fertilizers and pesticides.

Table 3.9: Institutional Linkages and Horticulture Producers

Hamlets/ Sources	*Trader in Farm Inputs*	*Local Villagers*	*Radio & TV*	*Government Department/NGO*	*Gram Pradhan*
Rajbhar	Eighty per cent of the information is received from the trader who sells seeds, fertilizers, pesticides and they trust that person.	Five per cent of information from local villagers	Not much trust on the information that they receive from radio, television and newspaper	Not much support or information from any government or NGO sources. Block agriculture office of five per cent relevance *Only water facility is available, no other facility by Government and NGO for getting loan etc. no subsidy is available.*	Nominated for different training programmes provides 10 per cent of the information to local farmers
Bangla Tola	*Main information received from the seed shop, the farmers being their permanent customers.*			*There is no support for horticulture produce by government or any other agency in terms of subsidies on various agricultural inputs such as seeds, fertilizers, and irrigation facility* *no financial support by bank or government to promote local horticulture produce*	
Morya hamlet, Lohta	The trader in seed, fertilzer and pesticide provides the maximum information.	Some information is available from one's own relatives and decisions are also based on one's own experience	Not mentioned	Some information is available at the block level office No support available	

Note: Women groups' views are in Italics. Collated from different villages.

Information disseminating government department are either non-existent or minor sources of support to horticulture producers. Those listening to radio and watching TV are able to get some information. Farmer to farmer exchange of notes is also common. Wherever, the village head is active and supportive, it is beneficial for the farming community because often the gram pradhan is nominated for different workshops and courses and attends official meetings.

3.16 HORTICULTURE PRODUCERS, MARKET DEMAND AND FOOD SAFETY

The producers in peri-urban Varanasi are in a position to identify those vegetables, which are of bad quality and often not safe in terms of food. The women and men participants during field research listed ways of identifying bad quality vegetables as indicated below and also stated factors, which make vegetable turn bad.

Some ways of identifying bad quality vegetables are listed below:

- For cauliflower, the colour turn pale yellow, the flower splits and a light bad odour emanates from the vegetable;
- Leaves of cauliflower when affected by insects thin down and also curl up;
- For spinach, the leaves turn yellow, the leaves curl around, become thin and transparent, in which capillaries can be seen, the leaves start decaying and bad odour emanates etc.;
- For okra, it becomes hard and the upper portion cannot be broken easily or it becomes soft and starts decaying; and
- Vegetable plants get burned and damaged with excessive use of chemical fertlizers.

3.17 HOW VEGETABLES TURN BAD?

Participants in different villages had some common views, which are indicated below:

- Over-dose of fertilizers and pesticides make vegetables go bad and even burn the plants.
- With blowing of the easterly wind the vegetable plants are generally attacked by insects, which damage crops.
- The impact of weather falls on vegetables. For example on spinach, which cannot tolerate excess heat or cold. The impact of cloudy days on cauliflower can cause damage when tiny black colour insects called "*Lahi*" develop.

- The impact of insects on all the three crops can be identified. The impact of insect on spinach results in curling of leaves and making of holes in them. For cauliflower, the insects go inside the flower, eat the leaves and make holes. For okra, the insects make holes in it.
- When dust accumulates on okra, a tiny insect called "*mite*" attacks its leaves and those harvesting such okra get an itching sensation from insect-bite, which can produce considerable discomfort.
- If harvested vegetables are kept for two days they turn pale, lose the shine and colour and turn soft.

Though there is awareness amongst producers about unsafe food, they are unable to overcome problems related to unsafe food. For example, though many have knowledge and experience that high dose of chemical fertilizers and pesticides damage crops, health and cultivable land, they are unable to get out of the such trap due to their low knowledge about other options and their feasibility. Hence, though they are aware that food is getting poisonous through use of chemical fertilizers and pesticides, they are not left with any option under the present circumstances. Based on their experience, the women have also stated that if milch animal is fed with vegetable fodder treated with high doses of chemical fertilizers and pesticides then the animal starts producing less milk. For washing vegetables harvested from the field, some villagers use clean water so as not to contaminate them. However, there are others who use dirty water and are least bothered/aware about the quality of water and the extent of contamination.

4

FOOD PREPARATION AND CONSUMPTION PRACTICES—FARIDABAD

In this section food preparation and consumption practices in peri-urban Faridabad have been focused upon. This is based on the interactive sessions in different villages with the consumers of vegetables in peri-urban Faridabad.

4.1 CONSUMPTION OF HORTICULTURE PRODUCE

In the peri-urban villages of Faridabad, different food items are consumed in different seasons. Main cereals like rice and wheat are consumed more in comparison to vegetables and fruits. However, milk consumption is generally on a regular basis in the villages and even the poor households consume milk once a day. Those vegetables taken raw are cucumber, tomato, carrot and radish, though they are also taken in cooked form. While carrying the produce from the field to home or market, some amount is consumed as raw by those engaged in it. Children consume more raw items than adults.

Earlier, many food items grew on common land and supported poor households. Now due to encroachment of common land for construction and cultivation, poor households have lost their access to the wild grown variety of vegetables.

About daily vegetable consumption the relatively better off have usually three meals—breakfast, lunch and dinner, though vegetable is not included in all the three meals. About one/two tablespoon/s of vegetable is/are consumed. As vegetables are spicy, a small quantity of cooked vegetable is enough for taking four-to five pieces of *chappati* along with *chutney* prepared from green/dry chilies, garlic and salt. Cauliflower is consumed in winter, okra in *chaumasa* (4 months) from its harvesting, spinach is consumed in winter (Kwar to Kartik) and not in summer for it produces heat in the body, according to village women.

4.2 REASONS FOR CONSUMING HORTICULTURE PRODUCE

In the peri-urban areas of Faridabad, the people think that horticulture items are needed for strength and these protect them from various diseases. One woman during a group discussion mentioned that ANM who visits the village frequently says that consumption of green leaves is essential for expecting mothers for strong eyesight of would-be child.

4.3 PERCEIVED NUTRITIONAL VALUE OF HORTICULTURE PRODUCE

The consumers from peri-urban villages such as Malerna, Sahupura, Sahapur Kalan and Sumper are of the view that spinach, carrot and radish are considered the best amongst vegetables in the village. Cauliflower, cabbage and okra are considered as city vegetables meaning thereby that they do not provide much strength to consumers. The villagers consider consumption of seasonal vegetables as a must along with cereals.

In other peri-urban villages such as Unchagaon, Chandawali and Majhgar, the consumers thought that cauliflower had no nutritional content (also see Table 4.1) as compared to spinach, which increases blood, helps in digesting food, provides strength and warms up human body. Both women and men share these views. However, the consumers said that during summer season they avoided spinach because it heats up the body and increases chance of heatstroke. The consumers thought that cauliflower and okra caused flatulence in their digestive system. In order to reduce flatulence, they cook cauliflower with potato. Though cauliflower is tasty they consume it in small amounts in order to reduce the incidence of gas. To reduce the gas content, the women use lemon during cooking. Table 4.2 reflects consumption patterns of vegetables in Chandawali village where men consume more of spinach and okra.

Table 4.1: Nutrition as Understood by the Community

Vegetable	*Nutrients as per cent*	*Losses*	*Why consumed*
Cauliflower	8 per cent	Flatulent 92 per cent	For Taste
Spinach	100 per cent		For Taste & Profit
Okra	10 per cent	90 per cent Flatulent	For Taste
Tomato	100 per cent		For Taste & Health

Note: Village: Majhgarh, Dated: 12-04-2001, Researcher: Saraswati.

The farmers do not consume vegetables keeping in view the nutritional value. They consume whatever is available from their field and sometimes from the market. Although cauliflower and okra can cause flatulence, these are taken for their taste. Children do not like spinach although this gives strength. Even adults do not like to eat spinach everyday. This vegetable is therefore cooked occasionally.

Table 4.2: Village Chandawali Jatwara: Consumption of Vegetables

Vegetables	*Men*	*Women*	*Children*
Spinach	Consumes 200 gms cooked vegetable	150-200 gms	Not more than 100 gms
Cauliflower	100 gms	100 gms	½
Okra	200 gms	150 gms	100 gms
Potato	250 gms	200 gms	200 gms

Source: From Field notes of Saraswati, Dated: 12-04-2001.

4.4 PURCHASE OF PRODUCE—SOURCE, REASON AND TIME

Often the consumers in the peri-urban villages of Faridabad purchase vegetables from nearby markets or from the vendor on the street. Most households try to manage vegetables from whatever they grow in their fields or kitchen garden rather than purchasing them from the market. The daily labourer requests the landowner for vegetables cultivated in the field. Village households, in need of vegetables, directly approach producers and get to buy fresh vegetables from the field at a cheaper price than the market price. Those vegetables not available in the village are purchased from the urban/ other markets, if there is a need. The villagers generally do not purchase vegetables from the market except for entertaining important guests or on special occasions.

4.5 ACCESSIBILITY OF POOR CONSUMERS TO HORTICULTURE PRODUCE

In the peri-urban areas of Faridabad, any vegetable when freshly harvested is available at a high price during the beginning of the season because it attracts buyers. Towards the end of the season, the prices fall and the same produce is sold very cheaply and often the producers suffer considerable loss. Cauliflower, at the beginning of the season, sells for Rs. 15 a piece but later becomes Rs. 5 a kg towards the end of the season.

The poor households consume vegetables, which are locally available to them free of cost, especially from the producer for whom they work. In case they cultivate their own vegetables, then they tend to keep a portion of it for their own consumption. In absence of vegetables, they take food with chilli chutney.

4.6 WAYS OF WASHING AND PREPARING HORTICULTURE PRODUCE

About ways of washing and preparing horticulture produce, the discussion was mainly with the women group since men did not show much interest. Women were comfortable in answering the questions because it is they who have the responsibility of washing and preparing vegetables. They said that all vegetables and green leaves were first cut and then washed. Vegetables are cooked with a lot of oil and spices. They do not eat much in terms of quantity of vegetables but prefer rich food. Most of the vegetables are cooked for long time and they lose their colour.

Many households, who retain a small portion of vegetables for household consumption, undertake further washing of vegetables. In case, there is a *kundi* located in the house, its water is used to wash vegetables for the second time. This is undertaken before household cooking and if no *kundi* is available then the vegetables are washed in large vessels. For cooking purposes, the women wash the vegetables more than once in order to clean them. Cauliflower, when cut into pieces, is washed in the pre-cooked stage for removal of insects and dirt. Okra is washed before cutting. Spinach is washed many times before cutting so as to clean it of sand and dust. Spinach is not washed after cutting because it is perceived that this process will remove the vitamins from the leaves.

4.7 CONSUMPTION OF HORTICULTURE PRODUCE AND COMMON PRACTICES

Horticulture produce is mostly consumed after cooking. Some women and girls eat raw cauliflower while they work in the cauliflower field. Some of them dry cauliflower and prepare vegetables from them in the off-season. Some also prepare *achar*/pickle with it. Okra and spinach are consumed after cooking. Those vegetables, which become dry, wilted and rotten, are not taken. The villagers prefer chilli *chutney* rather than taking vegetables, which have gone bad.

4.8 LEVEL OF AWARENESS OF CONSUMERS ABOUT FOOD SAFETY

The consumers of peri-urban Faridabad are aware of food safety, though more in terms of use of fertilizers and pesticide than pollution. During focus group discussion with both women and men groups, the following information came to light:

- If vegetables such as cauliflower and okra are left for three to four days, they get wilted and their taste deteriorates when cooked. So such vegetables are not used for cooking and are fed to livestock.
- Vegetables kept for long in humid environment become unfit for consumption, sometimes with fungus infection. The consumers are of the opinion that such vegetables cause diarrhea, stomachache and vomiting. Such vegetable is not fit for their livestock.
- Usually, cauliflower and okra can be insect-ridden, which are generally avoided from being consumed. Consumers belonging to very poor category eat them after removing the infected portions.
- Due to increased temperature in the environment, cauliflower becomes pale and scattered and become pungent in taste. Hence, the villagers prefer to feed it to their livestock.
- Okra is treated with a large dose of insecticide. Cauliflower and spinach are also treated with the same. Villagers from Chandawali are of the opinion that there is no harm in eating these vegetables the next day after washing them thoroughly.

During group discussion, some mentioned that pollution had no impact on plant but had impact on their health by causing breathing problem, while some said that it had impact on both—plant and human health.

4.9 ENHANCING SIZE OF VEGETABLES AND FOOD SAFETY

In two villages, the farmers revealed that they used to inject a medicine in the pumpkin and brinjal plants to increase its size and weight by twice or thrice. This helps them to get better price for the product. The farmers were not sure if such medicine had bad impact on human health. They were more concerned about getting good price for the vegetables. They admitted that the taste of such vegetables were not good and took a long time to get cooked. For their own home consumption, they always grew separate plants. On asking why they discriminated the city consumers, they replied that the city people enjoyed all the comforts at their cost (house on their land, get electricity and earn more). So there was no harm in extracting some money from them (by selling bigger vegetables and higher prices) to run their family.

The villagers mentioned that for consumers the food should be covered and kept in a safe place, away from insects and lizards. Any food item cooked well and consumed in time is safe.

4.10 SEWER WATER AND VEGETABLE GROWING— VILLAGE BADOLI

Towards the eastern side of the village, in 1990, sewer lines of colonies were constructed. The villagers have installed pump sets on the sewer chambers and are using this water to irrigate vegetable fields. During discussions, Smt. Sheela Sharma informed that there is bad odour emanating from the pressure cooker while cooking vegetables grown with sewer water. There is no such odour when vegetables grown with other water is cooked. In the same way, Shri Santraj informed that *chapattis* made out of wheat grown with sewer water also has a odd taste which is difficult to describe. The villagers have understood that with more factories coming up and more colonies being established, the water and air have become polluted. This has increased the incidence of respiratory diseases.

4.11 SOURCES OF INFORMATION ABOUT FOOD SAFETY AND NUTRITION

There is no such information available to consumers in the peri-urban area about food safety, except through television, radio programmes and discussion with friends. These are mostly relied upon.

—

5

FOOD PREPARATION AND CONSUMPTION PRACTICES—VARANASI

In this section, food preparation and consumption practices of consumers in peri-urban Varanasi have been described based on interactive sessions held in different villages.

5.1 SEASONAL AND DAILY FOOD CONSUMPTION OF HORTICULTURE PRODUCE

In order to study the food preparation and consumption practices among the villagers, the main items of food consumed by different sections of society were listed. The main items of food, especially vegetables, consumed by the villagers are as follows:

- Wheat (*chapatti*)
- Rice
- Pulse
- Potato
- Cauliflower
- Spinach
- Turai
- Brinjal
- Okra
- Lauki (gourd)

5.2 FREQUENCY OF FOOD CONSUMPTION

The following trends are prevalent amongst consumers in the peri-urban villages:

- Better-off groups consume vegetables almost daily, preferably in the evening.

- During the harvesting season, the frequency of consumption is four to five times in a week.
- During off-season, the poor households rarely purchase vegetable from the market. A few women purchase small quantities from village hawkers.

During off-season—summer and early rainy season, vegetables are expensive hence the villagers purchase only 250 gm potato for six persons. More frequently, the women grind 100 grams chilies and make paste (*chutney*) in lieu of vegetables.

5.3 AMOUNT OF VEGETABLES CONSUMED BY THE VILLAGERS

The amount of vegetables consumed is very low throughout the year. Only 500 gram to 1 kg of okra is cooked in a rich family of 6 members in one day. During off-season, the condition becomes very pathetic. Even rich do not consume vegetables more than 500 grams. The poor family consumes only a few pieces of potato (250 grams potato is cooked in a family of 6 members).

5.4 DAILY FOOD CONSUMPTION

As far as daily food consumption is concerned, the better off groups eat different vegetables such as lufafa, bhindi, potato, bottle gourd, bitter gourd, green peas, tomato, cauliflower, etc. from their own field. They eat potato throughout the year while green vegetables are taken depending on the season. They buy very few vegetables from the market excepting "parwal", which is not grown in their field:

- Pregnant women are given additional doses of fruits and vegetables and vitamin, beside normal food. Young girls eat normal food.
- Elderly women and men eat less but frequently and others serve them with fruits and vegetables.

Women groups while describing differences in food consumption amongst different socio-economic groups mentioned the following points:

- The poor consumer with low income consumes insufficient food during rainy season, when no work is available.
- The daily wager consumes sufficient rice, wheat and vegetables in all seasons. This group avoids purchasing off-season expensive vegetables from the market. Only potato is purchased.

- The better-off villagers, such as family of gram pradhan, consume sufficient food throughout the year. They purchase vegetables from the market—not more than 1 to 2 times in a week, when these are not available from their agricultural land.
- Most consumers, even from better off categories, are not in the habit of purchasing vegetables from the market. They prefer to consume only those vegetables grown on their own field.

About the role, which *bhindi*, cauliflower and *palak* play in daily consumption of better-off consumers, the following was noted from the field:

- *Bhindi* is used from Baisakh to Aghan, five times a week because it is produced on one's own land.
- Cauliflower is taken from Baisakh to Jeth and again from Aghan to Chet, three to four times a week.
- *Palak* is consumed daily in Baisakh and three times a week from Kuwar to Chet.

The worse off consumers consume twice a day— first time around 9-11 a.m. in the morning and second time around 7-9 p.m. in the evening:

- The children are given bare chapatti on-demand, whenever they are hungry.
- The pregnant/lactating/old are not given or demand any special diet.
- Usually the food is cooked in dung. There is no food cooked in between food or eaten.
- The food is cooked early morning, before women start other activities. In the evening, when all daily work is over, food is cooked for the second time.

5.5 REASONS FOR HORTICULTURE PRODUCE BEING CONSUMED

The following were the reasons stated by participants for consuming vegetables:

- It is a traditional food habit where one is used to consuming vegetables as supplement to rice/*chapatti* in the morning or with *chapatti* in the evening.
- Of the three vegetables, mostly those are consumed, which grow on one's own field because it saves on expenditure.

- Okra is generally easier to cook than the remaining two vegetables—cauliflower and spinach.
- Cauliflower is consumed for taste. The mixed vegetable—with potato, green peas and tomato—is very tasty.
- The spinach is consumed because it is easily available and also has medicinal properties. It provides strength.

5.6 PERCEIVED NUTRITIONAL VALUE OF HORTICULTURE PRODUCE

Many men and women participants were of the view that cauliflower has no vitamin and is consumed for its taste. As for spinach, many perceive that it has high level of vitamin, gives energy, improves eyesight, helps in producing blood in the body and can be cooked as a vegetable or mixed with pulses. For okra, it helps in producing blood, keeps stomach clean, provides vitamin and is tasty to eat.

An illustration from Maurya hamlet in village Bharthara is given in Table 5.1 where the men's group did a scoring exercise for comparing nutritional value of different vegetables. They regard palak as very nutritional, but find cabbage has no taste and gives out an odour.

Table 5.1: Scoring Exercise for Comparing Nutritional Value of Vegetables (1 = lowest score; 10 = highest score)

	Cauliflower	*Potato*	*Spinach*	*Cabbage*
Digestion	3	4	1	2
Vitamin	5	4	8	6
Gastric uses	8	6	1	2
Increases blood	5	4	8	6
Strengthens the eyesight	5	4	8	6

Participants: Dashuram Morya, Dukhi Morya, Hira Patel, Vishvanath Morya; dated 19-10-01; Place: Morya Hamlet, Village Bharthara; Facilitator: KK Singh.

It is clear from the above exercise that men participants of that hamlet are aware of the following facts:

- They are aware of the nutritive value of spinach,
- Spinach juice is beneficial for gastric related disorders,
- They recognize the nutritive value of cabbage, but dislike its taste, and
- They are ignorant of the nutritive value of cauliflower and potato.

5.7 PURCHASE OF PRODUCE—SOURCE, REASON AND TIME

Most vegetables are taken fresh from the field and mostly seasonal vegetables are consumed depending on whatever is produced in the field. Some vegetables are also purchased from the market. The following gives an general idea of the seasons in which the three study vegetables are procured from different sources.

In winter—Cauliflower is procured from home and also from the market; Spinach is procured from both home and market; Okra is not consumed.

In summer—Cauliflower is not consumed; Spinach is procured from both home and market; Okra—consumed from home production.

In rainy season—Okra is consumed from home production.

5.8 ACCESSIBILITY OF POOR CONSUMERS TO HORTICULTURE PRODUCE

The poor consumers own little or no vegetable cultivation and so they consumed less of it in their daily lives. They tend to consume cheap and often inferior quality of vegetables (about to decay or partially decayed) since they do not have enough to spend. The nutritional value of vegetables does not hold much meaning for them. They feel satisfied consuming some quantity of vegetables and cannot attend to the quality due to their low purchasing power.

Most consumers do not purchase spinach. They consume the produce from their own land. They consume it during winter. Cauliflower is consumed in winter. Some villagers purchase it if not grown on their land. During *khichari*, the villagers cook cauliflower, potato and green peas. On the other hand, okra is seldom purchased. The seasonal food consumption for very poor, poor and the better off sections of society differ as follows:

- The seasonal food consumption of the better off and poor people does not vary much in winter, when there are plenty of vegetables.
- The difference increases in the crisis months of Sawan and Bhado, when there is little or no income from other sources such as daily wage, *biri* rolling and *moti-mala* (bead necklace) preparation.
- Vegetables are consumed in the evening and the amount is meagre, in both the groups—about hundred grams of spinach/any green vegetables.
- The amount of vegetable consumed is more during harvest season.

5.9 WAYS OF WASHING AND PREPARING HORTICULTURE PRODUCE

With regard to the three study vegetables—spinach, okra and cauliflower—the following practices were common amongst women, as homemakers. The women participants mentioned that all vegetables, including the three study vegetables — spinach, cauliflower and okra — are washed properly.

Spinach is washed before making them into pieces. If the dust particles are more, they are also washed after cutting. After washing the vegetable, it is cut into pieces and re-washed and cooked, often mixing it with pulses or with some other vegetables.

Cauliflower is first cut into small pieces, then washed for taking out the insect/s. It is washed many times and/or boiled it with water and cooked with other vegetables.

Okra is Washed Before Making into Pieces

During discussion, it was clear that the method of washing vegetables is not linked with their nutritional preservation. The women do not have awareness about the concept of water-soluble vitamins. They wash to clean vegetables from sand, earth, insects and pests. They don't have the habit of washing hands and also don't know about cross-contamination of food.

Method of Cooking

In winter and rainy seasons, the quantity of oil and spices increases for vegetable curry they cook. In summer it falls:

- The method of preparation has the sole purpose of making the vegetable tastier. The women add various spices, more chilies, onion and garlic — almost all produced on their own land. The cooked vegetable is spicy, of which a small amount is enough to consume cereal — chapati and rice.
- Most of the women use cow-dung cake as fuel for cooking. Those who do not have livestock purchase it locally or buy wooden particles at cheap rate. A few use paddy husks and prepare food.
- Usually, vegetables are cooked in open vessel. The poor households cannot afford pressure cooker.

In the past, the village women used very little oil to cook their vegetables and hardly washed them. A part of vegetable was consumed as raw. They used cow-dung cakes as fuel for cooking.

Methods of Preparation of the Study Vegetables are as Follows:

Bhindi

- Usually vegetable is cooked dry.

- The *kalaunji* from *bhindi* is more expensive as it needs masala and more oil. The women cook it rarely.
- The dry vegetable is very common.
- *Bhindi* is not cooked as curry (rasedar).

Cauliflower

- Cauliflower is not cooked niral (without any combination). It is mostly cooked with potato.

Palak

- Cooked with potato.
- Cooked with pulses.
- Cooked with brinjal.

While cooking, the main concentration of the women is not retaining the nutrients but making the vegetable more spicy.

Some Observations by the Field Researchers

The washing practices of the vegetables are superficially related to removing dust and soil. The women are not aware of contamination to which the vegetables are exposed as shown by the following practices:

- The water containers are not covered.
- The containers are not washed.
- The hands are not washed always before handling vegetables, eg, washing, cutting in order to avoid cross-contamination.
- The soft vegetables, which need to be washed preferably by running water by gently rubbing them with hands, are washed in insufficient water.

Hygiene Standards During Cooking and Consumption

- The practices related to washing, cooking and consumption lack proper hygiene.
- The vegetables/rice are washed with the well water. The well is open, exposed to dirt.
- Practice of washing hands is not there.
- The food is not properly covered.

- The children do not wash hands before holding chapaties for consumption. Usually, children appear dirty with dust on their body. Nearby, there are livestock, dogs and goats.
- The women are not aware of the contamination process involved in washing, cooking and consuming.

5.10 CONSUMPTION OF HORTICULTURE PRODUCE

The women participants mentioned that okra is consumed in the form of *bhujia* and *kalaunji*, cauliflower as pickle, gravy vegetable and fried pakauri, while spinach is consumed as *bhujia* and vegetable. Moreover, women mentioned that they liked spinach because of its medicinal properties. It cures jaundice, increases blood, cools down body and digests food. The women named some preparations generally done by them:

- Dry preparation of okra, spinach and cauliflower.
- *Rasedar* (curry), with potato, green peas-cauliflower.
- Satpaita (with arhar/black gram/mixed arhar and black gram/ green peas with spinach.
- Kalaunji-okra.
- *Pakori-* cauliflower.
- *Achar* of cauliflower.
- Potato with spinach.
- Brinjal with spinach.

5.11 CONSUMERS' PERCEPTIONS ABOUT FOOD SAFETY

Not all consumers are aware or concerned about why consuming safe food is important and how to identify safety levels of food. The women generally go by thumb rules and tend to avoid unsafe food based on the following indicators:

- Stale food, which has been cooked a day or days in advance.
- Food, raw or cooked infested with insects, such as those found in cauliflower, okra, brinjal and others.
- Food, on which insecticides have been applied the same day.
- Cauliflower, which is pale-looking and loosely flowered.
- Bad odour emanating from spinach due to its gradual decomposition.

In this context, it is important to mention that the field researchers observed that in most study villages the cooking method was exposed to contamination, because frequent hand washing was not prevalent while cooking and the cooked food was not properly covered.

6

POLICY INFERENCES AND RECOMMENDATIONS

We have observed from the earlier chapters of this study that the small and marginal vegetable producers in the peri-urban areas of Faridabad and Varanasi are experiencing considerable difficulties in growing vegetables and sustaining their livelihoods gainfully under the prevailing circumstances. Under various constraints and deprivation, vegetable cultivation as an activity is ridden with problems with bleak future prospects. As an activity and a source of livelihood, an overall falling trend is visible with the younger generation—adults and adolescents not opting for such cultivation as a preference. There are major constraints and limitations related to local livelihoods mainly due to lack of institutional support and other adverse factors such as farming and infrastructure constraints, marketing constraints, lack of awareness and literacy etc. as described below.

In this context, it may be pointed out that in line with other sources of livelihoods, the livelihoods of small and marginal vegetable producers are dominated by a set of (or lack of) policies, institutions and processes, relevant to them, whether directly or indirectly. Such policies, institutions and processes are instrumental in defining contours of their livelihood options in producing and/or consuming vegetables and are critical in determining their access to resources of all types including financial resources, institutional support and applicability of rules, laws and institutional practices. Assessing such policies, institutions and processes from local perspectives and identifying institutional constraints in construction of livelihoods of small and marginal vegetable producers in the peri-urban areas are important exercises for informing future policy and practice.

6.1 FACTORS AFFECTING SMALL/MARGINAL VEGETABLE PRODUCERS AND CONSUMERS

Drawing from the earlier chapters of this study, we find that there are a range of factors, which adversely affect/weaken the livelihoods of the small and marginal vegetable growers in the peri-urban areas. Such factors are clustered below under the following heads:

- Agricultural Constraints;
- Infrastructural Constraints;
- Industrial Pollution and Regulation;
- Marketing Constraints;
- Lack of Appropriate Institutional Support;
- Lack of Access to Network/Information;
- Policy Changes favouring Rapid Urbanization;
- Low Literacy;
- Lack of Awareness on Food Safety Practices; and
- Lack of Women's Empowerment.

The above factors are described below.

Agricultural Constraints

Agricultural constraints such as small size of land, high cost of production, low productivity, pest attacks, low quality seeds, spurious pesticides, inclement weather and animal attacks — all operate as constraints for the marginal/small vegetable producers. The fast pace of using chemical fertilizers affect productivity of land. The farmers are observant enough and perceive with concern the adverse impact of increased fertilizer use on soil productivity as well as on the quality of crops/vegetables produced. However, they are unable to take action in absence of viable alternatives. Though application of insecticides to vegetables is on the rise, control of pests has become a real challenge with difficulties in tackling new pest attacks.

Infrastructural Constraints

Lack of irrigation facilities and availability of adequate water is a major constraint for growing vegetables. Many vegetables grown need assured irrigation. The better off families are able to arrange water through pumps through hiring or purchase. The poor vegetable growers with smaller sized land are unable to manage input costs though some have local tank water to help them out. Growing rain-fed vegetables is risky due to uncertainty of monsoons.

Industrial Pollution and Regulation

The quality of water available for cultivation is often a major constraint in peri-urban areas with water getting polluted due to industrial effluence and there is lack of awareness and also measures for treatment. The existing anti-pollution laws are flouted by the local industries and vegetable growers, amongst others, are affected directly as a result. There is little or no official attempt at surveillance of anti-pollution laws and other related regulations. Neither many local industries are willing to give out details to farmers of what items they produce, which include both intermediate and finished products. Many villagers observed in different villages about the industrial pollution – both in air and water, in terms of the smoke emitted by the local industries, the burning of chemical residues from plastic factories, dumping of waste materials into local canals, etc. Air pollution from nearby industries adversely affects vegetable production and in absence of institutional and legal support, the small and marginal vegetable producers in the peri-urban areas find it difficult to overcome such constraints.

Marketing Constraints

Vegetable cultivation requires more farm inputs in comparison to paddy and wheat and yield more income but involves higher risks. Profit is dependent on the right price of the vegetables in the market, though marketing is not easy in some villages due to the distance to be covered in approaching local markets. Though the produce is sold in the market there is no organized marketing or cooperative. The middlemen and traders are clever enough to quote low prices to the producers and thus rake in substantive profit for their own gain. Single-handedly, the farmers are in no position to influence the price quoted by the middlemen. The farmers sell individually to the traders and compete with each other. In this bargain, they often fail to get their cost price. At the start of the season, the vegetables are sold for good price but the price tends to fall towards the end of the season. Lack of cold storage facilities also reduces the chance of storing vegetable produce for long and provide opportunities to hedge price fluctuations.

Lack of Appropriate Institutional Support

A suitable form of institutional support in terms of supply of input at fair prices, dissemination of technical knowledge, loan facilities, marketing facilities and processing facilities, amongst others, are largely lacking for the small and marginal vegetable producers in the peri-urban areas. There is little or no institutional support for the promotion of horticulture produce. During serious damage and loss from vegetable production, most cultivators are unable to arrange loans from moneylenders in the village or the businessmen of the town due to the high rate of interest. The credit-worthiness and risk-taking ability of the small and marginal vegetable producers in the eyes of the financial institutions are low and negligible. Though there is support for big farmers from the financial institutions such as local banks, the options and choices for the small and marginal cultivators are virtually non-existent.

Lack of Access to Network/Information

For new varieties of seeds, imported seeds and agriculture inputs such as chemical fertilizers, pesticides and nutrients, the farmers mainly consult the local shopkeeper/trader selling agriculture inputs. Such informal consultation mostly relate to seed variety, application of fertilizers and pesticides. The farmers rarely approach the local agricultural research station—the Krishi Vigyan Kendra (KVK). Though the poor farmers can access crop-related information through radio and informal discussions in the village, the local shopkeeper/s of pesticides and agro-inputs tend to provide the major source of advice. There is no support system available for facilitating production of selected horticulture produce. Extension services are non-existent for the small and marginal producers. The extension staff generally visit the big farmers and also recommend their names for training in extension and capacity building. The latest entry on the scene are those of the seed companies which are specifically targeting the big farmers, training them and giving them support for experimenting with new seeds and new cultivation practices.

Policy Changes Favouring Rapid Urbanization

The small and marginal producers are required to cope with major policy-changes, especially the urban land-use policies such as acquisition of agricultural land for residential and industrial purposes, which is virtually imposed on them especially in Faridabad by Haryana Urban Development Agency (HUDA). At the beginning, the compensation for land acquisition by HUDA was marginal but has improved over time due to a court order. After the court order, the compensation for land given by HUDA has increased to Rs. 40 to Rs. 42 lakh per acre, which makee sale of land, more attractive as compared to crop/vegetable cultivation. Many people are selling their land in nearby villages in Faridabad and are, alternatively, acquiring new land located in the interior areas.

Rapid urbanization is also squeezing the agriculture dealers' market. The agriculture land is getting converted into residential land and there is a sizeable fall in dealers' business. For making up the loss in the market the agriculture dealer has started selling additional items such as animal feed. Few farmers come from a distance, of say 25 kilometers to buy agro-inputs while others come from a range of 8-10 kilometers.

Box 9: Traders in Agricultural Inputs

On our way back from village Chandawali in Faridabad, we interacted with a trading company in agricultural inputs near Subzi Mandi, Ballabhgarh, Faridabad. The shop deals in all types of seeds, fertilizers and other agricultural inputs. It has also started selling animal feed. The discussions were facilitated in the presence of the trader, a farmer and a representative from a reputed seed company. The trader said that they have training/meetings with the agriculture department in Ballabhgarh and Faridabad. During such training sessions, they sometimes get to learn new techniques and acquire knowledge about new items and processes. Some of their doubts are also cleared through such training sessions. Such sessions are generally held only once or twice a year.

The seed companies also organize their training sessions for traders and big farmers in their R&D offices. Here they stay for 2-4 days and are shown new varieties of items which they later try to grow on return to their villages. Such exercise is generally conducted once or twice a year. The seed companies work with dealers and distributors and call around 500 dealers from all over the country (India) along with the big farmers to their trial farms and show them the experiments. The farmers then go back to their own villages and try them out. The company also supports experimenting on the land of the big farmers and reports are firmed up later. The gestation period of such experiment is three years and the failure rate is about 20 per cent. An illustration of such failure is a particular instance of cultivating a hybrid variety of sunflower seed where with untimely rains the crop failed and there was also no demand for the product. This new venture therefore has failed to blossom. Those seeds, which outlived their shelved- life are taken back by the companies. There are different foreign companies supplying seeds from all over the world. These are prominently displayed on the shelves, whether from Korea, Thailand or elsewhere.

Krishi Vigyan Kendra (KVK) also has group/s of farmers whom they supported for trial of seeds. The trader is sometimes invited by KVK but generally KVK works directly with the farmers. The KVK does not sell seeds directly to the farmers. The farmers are closer to the traders and agriculture department than to KVK. KVK also gets seeds from the seed companies, gives trials and then recommends them to the farmers if found appropriate. KVK generally deals with small group/s of farmers.

All such inputs are channelled through the traders as both seed companies and KVK do not sell them to the farmers directly. The hybrid seeds sold by the companies have good yield but, unfortunately, these cannot be re-used because on re-use, the yield is either negligible or is not there. For some other seeds, it is a one-off yield when planted. The trader acquires new knowledge both from the agriculture department and the KVK. He also goes to the field and talks with the farmers to learn from them.

Source: From the field notes on Faridabad by Neela Mukherjee and Sumita Roy.

Low Literacy

There is lack of literacy, especially amongst the women. This hampers their empowerment process and better understanding of food safety practices. Whatever they have picked up is from the local ANM, while she makes her visits to the pregnant women.

Lack of Awareness on Food Safety Practices

Similarly, there is no source for acquiring information on food safety and nutrition. The women and men who are engaged in farming activities have little knowledge of different aspects of food safety. Information source related to preservation of nutrients by improving washing and cooking methods is almost non-existent.

Lack of Women's Empowerment

The women have limited knowledge on food safety practices. There is lack of institutional mechanisms to empower women in this direction. In terms of gender analysis, some important dimensions in this context are who does what work, how the work load gets shared, who is powerful and who decides on major aspects and who has access to resources. A look into the following gender aspects can provide some useful insights:

- Work and workload,
- Knowledge and skills,
- Decision-making, Access and control, and
- Power and status.

Work and Workload—In the villages studied, the women has the primary responsibility in household work, collecting and preparing food and taking care of children. Women take care of the family and spend considerable time with children than men. They are also more concerned with children's health and its maintenance. In vegetable production, both women and men are jointly engaged though women have higher share of workload. Even on a daily basis, women's workload is much more than men. The men have much spare time to play cards, drink alcohol and even gamble. Even when women are sharing work with men, their roles are defined either by tradition, social construction and societal pressures. In terms of daily chores and livelihood-related activities, a disproportionate burden is borne by the womenfolk.

Knowledge and Skills—Many women are illiterate and have less knowledge as compared to men. Women have more knowledge on household matters and better skills in farming practices, pest attack on vegetables, disease and crop patterns and animal care as compared to men who have better knowledge of the outside world and market.

Decision-making, Access and Control—Men tend to dominate decision-making and control cash. For small and marginal farmers, both women and men have access to surrounding land for growing vegetables. Women have limited access to financial resources and though they keep cash they cannot decide to spend it, except for small items.

Power and Status—In terms of social custom, women do not enjoy an equal status with men. The large number of children borne over-burdens her. The man is considered superior in all respects and generally command high dowry to be paid. There is considerable gender bias in terms of men wielding power in the sphere of governance, institutions and processes. The village *sarpanch* (head of the village) could be a man (or in case of a women *sarpanch*, her husband or father-in-law tend to wield the real power) and there are other men as political representatives at district and state levels. Similar is the situation with the line agency staff. The women's position is much inferior in both the states studied, and wife beating and domestic violence are quite common occurrence.

6.2 SELECTED RECOMMENDATIONS

One major aspect of the study is to identify possible ways of empowering the small and marginal vegetable producers (also as consumers of horticulture). It is to support them as a group of stakeholders in development for sustaining their livelihoods and their food safety practices. This, in turn, is expected to influence the food safety aspects of the consumers, who consume their produced food. There are three main routes to reduction/elimination of poverty of small and marginal vegetable producers in the peri-urban context, which can be constructed based on the following aspects:

- Changes in production patterns;
- Changes in consumption patterns; and
- Changes in livelihoods of the poor producers.

With regard to *changes in production patterns*, there are a few points, which can be listed. First, ad hoc and rampant use of fertilizers and pesticides is reducing crop productivity and soil fertility. New pests have emerged over time, which are difficult to treat. Knowledge of integrated pest management is absent amongst the small and marginal vegetable producers and neither do they have the comfort of experimenting with alternate ways of farming. The trader who is the main adviser on agro-inputs and what crops to grow is not always honest and efficient and is driven mainly by profit motive and market forces. The risks are entirely borne by the producers, where risk-taking capacity of the small and marginal producers is obviously low. So though there are changes in production patterns brought in by new seeds, agro inputs, contract farming and new technology, it is not reducing poverty and vulnerability of small and marginal producers to any considerable extent. Rather, the new technology and practices in agriculture are increasing the vulnerability of such producers and putting them at a disadvantage as compared to larger producers, who are better equipped in terms of resources, can undertake risk and face the market forces.

About *changes in consumption patterns*, flagging the nutritional aspects of food is important from the point of view of diet where poor households as consumers are unable to consume vegetables on a daily basis due to lack of purchasing power as compared to the better off consumers. The awareness about impact of chemical inputs in agriculture, which is considerably low, needs to increase amongst more villagers. The villagers need to be made aware about the impact of increased doses of pesticide, fertilizers, pests, dust and smoke emitted from nearby factories, which are presently not perceived as inflicting much of damage to human health. Some institutional mechanism is required to be set up at the village and block levels for dissemination of correct information in relation to consumption of unsafe food and its health hazard. Whatever information the villagers gather at present, is *ad hoc* and limited.

For bringing about positive *changes in the livelihoods of the poor producers*, it may be said that their vulnerability conditions need to be reduced through concerted efforts by local governance and pro-poor policy-making. Some of the steps towards sustainable livelihoods of the poor producers are discussed below:

6.2.1 Supportive Steps

Based on the principles of sustainable development, the following framework (Johnson and Wilson: 2000) provides useful indicators, based on which some supportive steps and policy recommendations have been drawn for the field study.

Box 10: Sustainable Development and Sustainability

Characteristics (or tasks) of sustainable development may include:

- Developing sustainable resource use,
- Building sustainable livelihoods,
- Reducing vulnerabilities,
- Enabling empowerment,
- Increasing equality, and
- Increasing self-reliance.

Sustainability may include:

- Continuity,
- An extended timeframe,
- The potential for activities to be self-supporting,
- The development of capacities,
- The realization of capacities through performance, and
- Learning as an integral part of developing capacities and assessing performance.

Source: Johnson, H. and G. Wilson, 'Institutional sustainability as learning', in Eade Deborah (2000), *Development and Management, Selected essays from Development in Practice*, Introduction by Tina Wallace, Oxfam GB in association with The Open University, p. 70.

Such recommendations emerging from the field study mainly point towards the following:

- Strengthening local sources of livelihoods by streamlining input supply,
- Establishing basic infrastructure facility, and
- Undertaking awareness/knowledge creation in education and health including food safety measures and best practices.

Many of the points below are indicative of the gaps in local governance and point towards necessary steps, which can be taken towards improving governance at the district level and at the block and the panchayat/village level. Drawing from Box 10 on sustainable development as given above, some steps towards supporting small and marginal vegetable producers and consumers include developing sustainable resource use; building sustainable livelihoods; reducing vulnerabilities; enabling empowerment; increasing equality and increasing self-reliance.

Some specific recommendations are as follows:

Reducing Vulnerabilities: Stabilizing Market Prices of Vegetables

Stabilizing vegetable prices would constitute a step towards reducing vulnerabilities. The movements of vegetable prices in the market are highly erratic depending on various factors. When the prices of vegetables in the market start to fall, the vegetables start to rot. For example, one sack full of carrots, for which Rs. 50 was spent in harvesting, washing and transporting, fetched only Rs. 30 in the market thereby inflicted loss to those producers. There is considerable loss to the farmers when the prices fall and vulnerabilities increase when prices tend to fluctuate. The farmers and traders are of the view that government should fix minimum selling prices for vegetables similar to those of rice and wheat.

Reducing Vulnerabilities: Planting Vegetables during Off-season is High Risk

The traders are of the opinion that growing vegetables during off-seasons is a high risk activity for the small and marginal producers. The small and marginal producers, with less resources and risk-taking capacity, find it difficult to cope with as compared to the big producers. Vegetable cultivation is less risky during the seasons rather than the off-season. The traders generally advise farmers to grow vegetables during appropriate seasons.

Reducing Vulnerabilities: Growing New Crops

The traders are of the opinion that small and marginal producers should experiment with growing new crops such as herbs, *elaichi*, ginger, turmeric, *jowar* and others whose markets look promising and prices are remunerative. However, availability of seed for such items could constitute a problem.

Enabling Empowerment: Information Dissemination

The farmers feel the need for proper information dissemination. They suggest that priced booklet should be made available at the seed shop. The booklet could contain information about best practices for profitable cultivation, marketing networks and prices, information on funding agencies for getting soft loans and subsidies etc.

Enabling Empowerment: Other Measures

Institutional support and good governance are required for strengthening the capacity of the small and marginal producers of vegetables in the peri-urban areas. Some policy do-ables for empowering small and marginal vegetable producers include:

(i) Demonstration/pilot schemes at the local level in the peri-urban areas to help in propagating good and efficient practices for vegetable cultivation;
(ii) Large-scale propagation of integrated pest management techniques, compost-making methods, and organic cultivation practices for producers to ultimately support food safety practices;
(iii) Making available enough water for irrigation and uninterrupted electricity, especially for those growing vegetables in the peri-urban areas;
(iv) Making available financial support to promote local horticulture, especially for small and marginal horticulture producers, whether through banks or cooperatives;
(v) Making available agricultural inputs such as seeds and fertilizers at fair prices and on a regular basis for sustaining regular supply of agriculture inputs;
(vi) Supporting establishment of food processing enterprises with appropriate incentives — establishment of storage facilities like godowns along with cold storage can be set up at different locations in consultation and collaboration with horticulture producers;
(vii) Means of increasing off-farm employment opportunities needs to be explored;
(viii) Implementing anti-pollution laws for setting up of proper drainage facilities for channeling polluted water and its treatment by the industrial units and proper tackling of those industries/persons flouting anti-pollution laws;

(ix) Raising awareness for improving food safety practices including sanitation practices for better harvesting, processing and handling of vegetables and those related to preventive health aspects;

(x) Encouraging vegetable producers to form vegetable farmers' cooperatives and strengthening their institutional linkages with service providers such as input suppliers, banks, extension agents, marketing networks and others;

(xi) Arranging and supporting access to information through printing information brochures along with other literature and providing interactive multi-media facilities at suitable contact point/s; and

(xii) Creating niche areas and developing markets/brand names for organic vegetables and other produce. Supporting value addition through downstream processing of vegetables and providing facilities and scope for preservation/packaging of sliced vegetables and their trade. On the consumption side, selected initiatives are required from the governance side to promote food safety practices in vegetable consumption

(xiii) Raising awareness in nutrition and promoting health education and knowledge amongst women; and

(xiv) *Some Steps to Support Disadvantaged Women* – Identifying ways of empowering disadvantaged women in terms of the following:

- Disseminating improved food safety practices including demonstration sessions to promote better cooking practices for preservation of the nutritive value of the vegetables;
- Empowering disadvantaged women in terms of human, physical and financial resources for bettering sources of livelihoods;
- Supporting women's nutrition and health services where inputs in nutrition and health education can help to raise awareness and knowledge amongst women. For young girls and boys such inputs need to be included in school curricula;
- Supporting women's savings, credit and marketing groups for income generating activities;
- Supporting women's training in improved vegetable cultivation practices, harvesting and processing, animal husbandry, sanitation and other related topics; and
- Improving her human capacity, confidence level for providing her better social status and voice in the family and the society at large. Establishing women producers' groups on the principle of self-help and encouraging home-based and other enterprises through vocational training to strengthen such groups.

6.3 AREA/S FOR CONTINUOUS ACTION-LEARNING

Action-learning could constitute an integral part of supporting small and marginal producers whether in crops or vegetables. We have already studied how lack of support system is adversely affecting the livelihoods of such producers. It is important to provide institutional support in terms of action-learning, which has been described as an iterative process that involves learning how to innovate, be adaptive and deal with complexity and turbulence (Carley and Christie:1992). The small and marginal producers in the peri-urban areas are faced with complex decision-making processes with regard to their production space, techniques, lack of infrastructure support, policy context and vulnerabilities due to market prices, inferior agriculture inputs, etc. and other constraints.

Such action-learning could take place at different levels for both the support institutions and the small/marginal producers involved in such learning process:

- Learning in depth so that particular practices are fully understood and then change, adaptation and/or improvement; that is to say virtuous circles of learning and practices get facilitated.
- Learning in breadth, which involves performance assessment on a broader basis.
- Transferability of learning, when purpose of learning is not restricted to the improvement of a particular area but to all aspects of life. This is not only about personal, managerial life-skills, or even about organizational learning, but also the transferability of the learning process to new situations.

6.3.1 Future Action/Field Research

A total of nine peri-urban villages of Faridabad district and six peri-urban villages of Varanasi district have been covered, which clearly indicate that future field research could have larger samples. In the context of action-learning relating to poor producers and food safety issues, future directions in action/field research could include support towards assessing information needs of small and marginal farmers and preparation and dissemination of educative audio-visual materials—ICT materials on food safety practices and related issues. For this purpose, it is important to undertake participatory need assessment exercises, which can help to indicate whether such material will prove useful or not for the target audience—the producers and/or the consumers. Based on the results of such need assessment exercises, decisions could be taken on "why" and "how" aspects of such material and its preparation by appropriate agencies.

Results from the field also indicate that the impacts of air pollution and water pollution are interrelated. Water as a source of pollution is more visible to the farmers than air as a source of pollution. From the farmers' perspective, water pollution and air pollution are closely related. However, for the present study the focus was on food safety and not water pollution. Hence, in order to have a complete picture on food safety and for improving food quality, it is essential that fieldwork focuses on both air and water pollutions and their interface. The study is more in lines with exploratory research. The issue of food safety is important and the action-learning related to small and marginal vegetable producers and their livelihoods and consumption needs to move on and the results be fed into policy-making and practice with wide dissemination, sharing and feedback amongst different stakeholders of development.

Annex 1

FIELD INQUIRY

During field inquiry the local communities were approached for conducting both exploratory and topical rounds of inquiry. The methodology for the field inquiry was based on the methods and principles of Participatory Rural Appraisal (PRA) and Participatory Learning and Action (PLA). Though the principles of PRA were the foremost in deciding the basis of research, the approach adopted for field research was that of Participatory Rapid Rural Appraisal (PRRA). "PRRA is a variation of PRA, which is widely used where information is required by external agencies but must be expressed by the communities themselves in their way and with their own emphasis" (UNDP's 1996 Report on Human Development in Bangladesh, A Pro-Poor Agenda, Volume 3, 1996). The process adopted for the fieldwork was that of interactive sessions based on PRA/PLA with groups of women and men and mixed groups as well.

Field inquiry for the project included the following methodological aspects:

(i) Exploratory overviews,
(ii) Topical probing,
(iii) Probing for gap filling,
(iv) Validation of results, and
(v) Sharing with different stakeholders.

Exploratory overviews and topical probing were undertaken in a total of 15 villages with nine study villages in Faridabad and six study villages in Varanasi during 2001-03 and other aspects were included during the course of fieldwork for "deepening" of such field research. The PRA/PLA methods applied during the fieldwork included a range of tools and techniques. Some of the field methods and the aspects probed are indicated below in Table A1.

Table A1: Field Methods and Topical Inquiry

Methods Applied	*Aspects Probed*
Participatory mapping	Locations, setting of the village, social groups, crops/vegetables grown, infrastructure etc.
Semi-structured interviews	Conducted on all aspects of the check list
Historical transect of selected vegetables	Provided an historical background of cultivation of crops and vegetables.
Crop calendar	Provided an overview of the crops/vegetables grown throughout the year.
Seasonal calendar of food consumption	Provided seasonal picture of food/vegetable consumed in different months
Daily food calendar	Provided picture of food/vegetable consumed on a daily basis
Gender workload calendar	Calendar depicted women's and men's workload in terms of different activities
Criteria listing for selected vegetables	A set of criteria was used for comparing different vegetables produced/consumed
Matrix scoring of selected vegetables	Different vegetables/crops produced/ consumed were compared against a set of criteria including discussion related to "why", "how", "how much", by which group etc.
Preference ranking/scoring of selected vegetables	Selected vegetables ranked/scored according to preferences of producers/consumers
Pie charts on vegetable production/consumption	Share of selected vegetables in production or consumption
Oral history	The participant narrated orally the history of producing selected vegetable/crop
Case studies	Case study of a household/group producing selected vegetables/crops and their experience and lessons learnt

Sampling : Varanasi Study Villages

A list of villages was prepared with the help of the Botany Department of BHU where selected vegetables such as cauliflower, okra and spinach were grown for livelihoods' purposes. Villages from two blocks, namely, Kashi Vidyapith and Arajilines were selected in the District of Varanasi. Villages Maraw, Lohta and Bharthara were selected from the Kashi Vidyapith block cultivating spinach and cauliflower while village Parampur was selected from the Arajilines block located in the okra cultivating belt. Village Sundernagar and village Chandpur were also included as study villages. Only those hamlets within the villages were selected which were practising vegetable cultivation.

Criteria for Selection of Area and Villages

The criteria for selection of village/hamlet/area were as follows:

- Those areas close to sites where the earlier study on air pollution was done;
- Those villages producing different horticultural produce under consideration;
- Coverage of villages/hamlets where different communities and castes reside e.g. Hindus, Muslims, Dalits etc.;
- Coverage of villages located near roadside and those further interior;
- Coverage of villages, both large and small;
- Coverage of villages located close to industrial sites and other areas; and
- Coverage of villages having/not having farming as main livelihood.

Sampling : Faridabad Study Villages

The field researchers selected villages close to the industrial belt of Faridabad, amongst those, which were studied during the earlier project on air pollution and crop yield. All the villages considered grew vegetables. However, the amount of cultivation of the vegetables under study — cauliflower, okra and spinach — varied. Both producer and consumer groups were available in the villages. The distance of the villages from Ballabhgarh is less than eight km. The criteria for selection were as follows:

- Previous peri-urban villages, which were selected earlier for the DFID project on air pollution and crop yield;
- Those villages, which are important peri-urban areas for vegetable cultivation;
- Coverage of those villages, which have horticulture as one main source of income and produce amongst the three vegetables, cauliflower, okra and spinach;
- Coverage of villages closer to industrial areas and also further away;
- Villages near road side and away; and
- Both large and small size villages.

The approach in the study villages was in terms of interacting with groups of local women and men who were horticulture producers and consumers. The timings for the meetings/interactive sessions were decided in consultation with local people. Interactions with the sample group/s were held on a random basis. In some cases during transect walk, separate discussions were held with individual farmers growing vegetables in their fields. Separate group discussions were held with women groups.

For peri-urban villages Badoli and Budhayna studied in the last round of field inquiry, the sampling was based on multiple criteria such as vegetable cultivation, distance from Ballabhgarh and livelihood patterns as indicated above. Vegetable cultivation in the two villages differed widely in terms of background of the cultivators. Whereas in village Badoli, the migrants were cultivating vegetables in village Budhayna the local residents were engaged in such cultivation. Though both the villages Badoli and Budhayna were growing vegetables, the amount of cultivation of cauliflower, okra and spinach differed amongst the villages. Altogether nine villages of Faridabad district and six villages of Varanasi district were covered during fieldwork in 2001 and in 2002.

Each round of fieldwork in the study villages was planned in such a way so as to add value towards broad-basing findings from research inquiry, "deepening" of topical probing and validation of field findings. Understanding the existing information, advice, governance issues and support system for horticulture consumers was researched in each round. The other aspect of present research study was to probe into social analysis in terms of issues related to food quality, food consumption and sustaining livelihoods. This was done for selected number of villages though not for all. Scanning of such data for inter-group variations was later taken up with emphasis on washing, preparation and consumption practices.

During field inquiry, vegetable cultivation as a source of livelihood vis-à-vis other sources was probed through interactive sessions with both groups and households for gaining insights into local community perspectives. Groups of local women and men also analysed issues related to consumer safety and patterns of purchasing/production, preparation and consumption of vegetables. The vulnerability context of those poor groups growing and consuming vegetables in the peri-urban areas, was also studied. At the intra-household level, selective probing was undertaken into the gender dimensions of food production and consumption of different poor groups, which yielded meaningful results. Fieldwork helped in learning about post-harvesting techniques and stages of processing in the food chain, especially for the consumers as stakeholders. The sources of advice and support available to poor consumers and producers of horticulture were also researched upon. Fieldwork also covered validation and cross-checking of data and gap filling.

Rounds of Field Inquiry

During the first round of field inquiry to Faridabad in March 2001, three peri-urban villages were covered, namely, Unchagaon, Sagarpur and Chandawali. In the second visit to Faridabad in end-March peri-urban villages covered were Malerna, Sahupura, Sahapur Kalan and Sumper. The third round of fieldwork was undertaken in April 2001 in peri-urban villages of Faridabad — Unchagaon, Sagarpur, Majhgarh and Chandawali. In April

2002, two more peri-urban villages were studied, namely, Badoli and Budhayna. The first round of fieldwork in Varanasi was undertaken in October 2001 in peri-urban villages Maraw, Parampur, Lohta and Bhartara. The second round of fieldwork was held at Varanasi in November 2002 to cover village Sundernagar and village Chandpur. A validation round in early 2003 was held for selected Faridabad locations. Approximately, 358 participants (200 men and 158 women) were interacted with during fieldwork in different locations at Faridabad and Varanasi, of which, 158 (44 per cent) were women participants. Those people are not included who came off and on for the PRRA sessions and also the curious on-lookers.

Fieldwork

Fieldwork was a combination of both exploratory and topical approaches to village study. Of the nine villages covered in Faridabad, four were covered in terms of gaining "overviews" and in the rest of the villages fieldwork was done for having deeper insights into selected hamlets, which were growing vegetables. In Varanasi, only four villages were covered in terms of in-depth inquiry while there was rapid assessment for two villages. For selection of hamlets in different villages, considerable care was taken for comparing different hamlets within any selected village and taking up those hamlets, which grow more vegetables.

Amongst those cultivating vegetables, selection of hamlets was made in a manner where other criteria such as caste, social/ethnic group were considered so as to broaden the picture in terms of social criteria. Based on such analysis of difference, the objective of selecting hamlets was aimed at getting differential picture rather than any uniform or homogenous picture. In order to flag gender perspectives, those researchers with focused approach and in-depth probing did their research interactions in gender-specific groups.

For better interaction with local groups, field researchers conducted sessions with women groups during evening, especially in Faridabad. The women groups had little time to spare during the day. Due to gradual rise in day temperature and unbearable heat during the summer months of 2001, it became difficult for farmers to interact during daytime. Hence, interactive sessions in the evening became important.

For selection of hamlets in different villages, considerable care was taken for comparing different hamlets within any selected village and taking up those hamlets, which grow more vegetables. The approach to the village groups of producers and consumers in the study villages was in terms of interacting with farmer groups who cultivated vegetables and those who also consumed them. The timings for the meetings were decided by the farmer groups. Interactions with the sample group/s were held on a random basis. In some cases during transect walk, separate discussions were held with individual farmers growing vegetables in their fields. Separate group discussions were held with women groups in order to flag gender issues.

There was considerable heterogeneity amongst the field researchers in terms of training, discipline, focus, approach, methods, experience, etc. Such heterogeneity amongst the field researchers helped in mutual learning experience, sharing and offsetting biases. However, it also had its impact on the quality of research where those with more experience in PRA and also the "*Air Pollution and Crop Yield*" Project, brought in their insights and lessons that they had learnt in the earlier projects.

Annex 2

PROFILES OF STUDY VILLAGES IN PERI-URBAN—FARIDABAD

Peri-urban villages: Unchagaon, Chandawali, Majhgarh, Badoli, Budhayna, Sahupura, Malerna, Sumper, Sahapur Kalan

Unchagaon

The population of this village is about 6500 comprised of both small and big farmers. Vegetable farming is done on 400 *kilas* (acres) of land, which is about 80 per cent of the total land available. Out of the total population, 25 per cent are landless and earn their livelihood as labourers, 25 per cent have one *kila* or less of land, 30 per cent have two to three *kilas* of land, 10 per cent have land more than five *kilas*, and the remaining 10 per cent have more than 10 *kilas* of agricultural land.

Unchagaon is located 4 kms southeast of the district headquarter office of Faridabad and is 2 kms from the Ballabhgarh main road. Out of the total 935 families settled in this village, 600 belong to the Sainis, 100 to Dalits, 70 to Jats, 65 to Ahirs and 100 to other castes. The standard of living and attire are ordinary. Although the condition of women is satisfactory, the entire responsibility from household to agricultural activity is on them. The womenfolk are therefore extremely busy and cannot spare any time for conversation/discussions. The younger girls also help their mothers in all household chores as well as fieldwork. There is awareness about education and till the primary stage both boys and girls attend school. The number of girl students gets reduced by the 10th level and by 12th level the number is practically halved. This is because of household responsibilities as well as early marriages. There are schools in the villages but mostly boys acquire higher education. Due to the proximity of the industrialized areas, a large number of the populace work as construction workers, contractors and security guards.

Chandawali

Chandawali village is situated on the Mohna road, 6 kms from the district headquarters of Faridabad and 4 kms southeast of Ballabhgarh industrial area. People live in their houses around the fields. Towards the west is the Agra canal. The water is murky as all the waste of the town is drained into this canal. Even the dirty water of the leather factories of Ghaziabad is emptied into this canal. The canal meets the Yamuna river and beside the canal there is another drain carrying dirty water.

The population of the village is comprised of Jats, Ahirs (Yadav), Gujjars, Sainis, Brahmins, Koli Rewari, Dhobi, Kumhars, Bania, Hathi Barai and Muslims. In this village with population of about 4500, land for agricultural use is 2400 bighas, out of which 60 bighas are cultivated and 40 bighas are inhabitated. The villagers do agricultural work. Short crops like spinach, methi, etc. are cultivated by Sainis. The Jats and Gujjars are engaged in bigger crops. The Dalit (*Chamar*) households, which have agricultural land, cultivate okra and cauliflower. This village is already affected by pollution. Through air pollution and the dirty water of the canal, pollution is on the rise. Different diseases like cough, malaria, small pox, etc. have taken on a dangerous form. Agriculture is the main *source* of livelihood but people also work in industrial areas. The caste system is still visible in the village. Primary education is 90 per cent, junior schooling is 60 per cent, high schooling is 40 per cent and higher education is restricted to 10 per cent. Out of the total agricultural land, 60 per cent is utilized for vegetable farming, 30 per cent for mix of vegetable and wheat and 10 per cent for cattle feed — barsam, jawar etc.

The main source of livelihood of the villagers of Chandawali is agriculture, supported by service and buffalo rearing. People earn extra income through sale of buffalo milk and 3-4 per cent of the population sell vegetable on retail in the market, or on commodity basis from the godowns. The commission work of sale of godowns in the market can fetch 15-20 thousand rupees a month. Discussions were done in Chandawali village, the village of Gujjars, Munjeri Road, Chatri and information was received from the Gujjar community. Their traditional occupation is buffalo rearing. They had even tried vegetable farming on agricultural land but due to inexperience, suffered losses from okra and cauliflower crops despite such crops being profitable for other communities. They abandoned such risky agricultural ventures and have started cultivating potato, brinjal, chilly, gourd, kankri, bitter-gourd, etc.The number of buffalos reared by Gujjar families ranges from 4-5 to 25 to 30 buffaloes. The Gujjars sow grains in their land and grow food for self-consumption and also fodder for the cattle. This process does not require them to spend much time on agricultural activity.

The Jatwara hamlet of Chandawali village

Chandawali village is located on Mohna road, 4 kms southeast of Ballabhgarh industrial area. Of 5000 population, 1500 are from Jat community and out of 300 acres of agricultural land, 100 acres are cultivated by Jats. They cultivate long and big vegetables with high yield. The main source of income is agriculture, animal rearing and government/non-government jobs. The socio-economic condition of Jat community is based on animal rearing as their traditional livelihood. Those with more land pursue agriculture depending on the benefits available to the family and the animals.

The Jat women do agricultural work along with the household work and animal rearing. Being located near a town, the households of the Jatwara show a mix of town and village culture. The effects of pollution are also visible in Chandawali village. Ten per cent of the population work in government and other offices. But even those in service have to be engaged in agricultural activity for fear of being called 'good for nothing'.

The Jats have a lot of agricultural land. They cultivate paddy, wheat, jowar, jai, barsam and vegetables like onion, potato, cucumber, kankri, chilly, brinjal, etc. Cauliflower and okra were grown till about four years ago and having suffered losses, other vegetables giving more profits were taken up. The Jat community engages labourers for much of the agriculture-related work.

Majhgarh

Village Majhgarh is located adjacent to Chandawali village, 6 kms southeast of Ballabhgarh industrial Area. The population of the village is made up of Gujjars, Jats, Pandits, Kolis, Jogis, Balmikis, Dalits, Kumhars, Khatis, Seths, Lohars, Bairagis, etc. Out of the 1300 families, the Jat community is predominant having 800 families followed by Gujjars with 150 families. Others are of lesser number. The total population is about 7000. There is a lot of consciousness about education. The educated people after completing graduation cultivate field as no jobs are available. Education is 100 per cent for primary level, 90 per cent for junior level, 50 per cent for high school and inter-level and 10 per cent for BA level. There are people with post-graduate qualification, MBBS, engineering degrees also up to four per cent including women. However, there is ome difference between education amongst men and women. The education begins for boys and girls together, but as soon as girls reach an age when they can mange the household, the percentage of education amongst girls goes down. At marriageable age, the percentage reduces by 50 per cent.

The main occupation of the population in the village is agriculture and animal rearing. People also work in government industrial areas. Out of the total population, 5 per cent are drivers, 20 per cent are labourers, two per cent are shopkeepers. The people in jobs also give full attention to agriculture. The farmers in Majhgarh village cultivate all varieties of vegetables but short crops like spinach, methi, dhania, etc. are less. People also cultivate cauliflower but okra is more popular as it is felt that there is less cost and more yield, despite the difficulty in plucking okra.

Badoli

Village Badoli is situated in rural Faridabad, 200 meter away from Police check post near the sector by-pass road. The Agra canal is in the east the village, in the west lies village Bhatola, in the north is village Budhayna and in the south is the NTPC plant. The village has a total of 431 households, with a total population of 3754, of which 2050 are males and 1704 are females. The dominant caste in the village is that of Gujjar followed by scheduled caste, barber, Muslims and Brahmins. The main source of livelihood is livestock rearing. Other sources are farming, government service, non-government service, grocery shop, wage labour, etc. The main market for the village is that of Faridabad.

In village Badoli, vegetables are being grown by seven migrant families from Uttar Pradesh and Bihar. The seven migrant households have taken temporary lease of land and stay in makeshift huts near the fields for purpose of growing vegetables. Amongst vegetables, mostly cauliflower is grown in the Rabi season, while some spinach is also grown. As a coping strategy in case of failure of their vegetable crops, they trade in vegetables by buying it from *Mandis* and selling it at the weekly market of Faridabad housing colonies.

In this village, the dominant caste is Gujjar and their main source of livelihood is livestock rearing and milk production. The other households residing in this village are also engaged mainly in milk production, which is their prime occupation followed by farming. The local residents of this village perceive vegetable growing as more labour-intensive than livestock and milk-related activities. They also think that for growing vegetables one needs more hands for work, which is expensive and not always available. They are also of the opinion that livestock rearing and milk production have a higher status while vegetable growing has a much lower status and hence they are reluctant to do vegetables and leave it for migrants to cultivate it.

In the eastern side of the village, some pump sets have been installed on the sewer lines of Faridabad housing colonies for drawing sewer water for irrigating fields including vegetables. One village woman by the name of Sheela Sharma said that the vegetables grown in her field with sewer water emit a foul smell when cooked in pressure cooker in her home. This smell is not there for vegetables grown with normal water. Mr. Santraj, a resident of the same village, said that there is a world of difference between the chappati prepared from wheat grown by sewer water and that grown with normal water. Some residents also mentioned that because of establishment of factories and housing colonies both air and water have become polluted and incidence of cough and breathing problems have increased.

Budhayna

Village Budhayna is located in the municipal area of Faridabad and grows vegetables. In Budhayna, vegetables are grown in 70 per cent of the land during the Rabi season. The main vegetable grown is cauliflower followed by spinach. There are 412 households in the village with a total population of 3,484, where 1,811 are female and 1,673 are male. The dominant caste is Gujjar, followed by scheduled castes, barber, Muslim, potter and Brahmin. There are four *Muhallas* in the village by the names of Kouyya muhalla, Pohoula muholla, Alli Puriyan muhalla and Miya muhalla. During field inquiry it was found out that vegetables were being grown by 15 households in Kouyya muhalla, while Pohoula muhalla had seven households, while the rest of the two muhallas had four households each, growing the vegetables. The gross cultivated area under vegetables was 92.7 acre, of which 53.5 acre (57.7 per cent) was being grown by Kouyya muhalla alone. Hence the same muhalla was selected for field inquiry. In Kouyya muhalla, there is 143.6 acre of agricultural land and 15.40 of residential area. This muhalla is in the southeast of the village. There are a total of 154 households residing here.

Sahupura

In village Sahupura there are 350 households and 1,200 population with 1,200 voters in the village. Regarding caste composition, there are 50 Brahmin households, 70 Jat households and some households from Muslims, potter, carpenter, dalit and barber. From this village at least 50 per cent of people go to Ballabhgarh town (5 km away) for work. Soil type is do moth and water availability is normal. There is 650 acres of land in this village. It has 30 tractors and 50 tube-wells. In this village Haryana Urban Development Authority (HUDA) has acquired land since May 1998. Cultivable land has reduced by 50 per cent due to road construction, house construction and now HUDA.

Pollution is felt from northwest wind blowing from Malerna and Ballabhgarh. In this village, 90 per cent farmers cultivate main crops such as paddy and wheat, while small farmers cultivate vegetables. The big farmers mentioned that wheat and paddy require less attention and manual labour and at the same time has an assured market price. On the other hand, vegetable cultivation require more attention and more labour and often do not get the right price. In 1999 and 2000, all those who invested in potato and onion could not get the investment price in the market and many had to dump their produce in Agra canal. Therefore, farmers hesitate taking risk. Those who cultivate vegetables do a variety such as cabbage, cauliflower, spinach and okra. The soil type is suitable for all kinds of vegetables and even water availability is not a problem. About 10 years back the vegetable cultivation increased up to 15 per cent of total cultivation but now it is just 5 per cent.

Malerna

Village Malerna is close to village Sahupura and is only five km from Ballabhgarh. There are 350 households in this village and the total population is about 1,768. People from different castes such as Yadav, Brahmin, Jat, weaver, dalit, kohli, potter, etc. live here. People reside in caste-based clusters. Mostly Yadav and Jat cultivate vegetables. Soil is do moth and the water is hard. There are 40 tube-wells in the village and 20 tractors. This village is electrified since 1970. Thermocol factory has come up since 10 years and pollutes the air of that area though the factory got closed down when the field research was on. The village is prone to pollution from Faridabad factories when wind blows.

Vegetable cultivation is relatively less in the village. Farmers prefer to grow main crops such as paddy, wheat and mustard. Uncertain markets and high investment discourage many from cultivating vegetables. Damage by stray cows is also another problem. Those who cultivate vegetables grow beet root, carrot, radish, potato, etc. as they do not have to protect them from cows. Vegetables grown such as cabbage and spinach get marks on the top of the leaves and even holes are found in them due to pollution. In case of cauliflower, it gets black patches on the top and grows small.

Since ten years, production of other vegetables started in the village. About 20 years back the household consumption was dependent on own production but this trend changed with markets growing at close proximity to the village. Earlier, exchanging of food items was more prevalent with households though now this has reduced considerably as selling produce in the market has become more attractive.

Sumper

Village Sumper is 6 to 7 km away from Ballabhgarh. In this village there are 320 households with a population of 1,714 and number of voters as 800. The village has different castes residing in it such as Rajput, Dalit, Brahmin, Barber and Saini, who cultivate vegetables, Baoria and Gadaria who raise livestock. There are 160 Rajput households in the village, which are the landowners. In this village about 75 per cent of the population depend on agriculture and 25 per cent on non-agricultural activities.

Cultivable area in the village is 600 acres. There are 20 tractors, 30 tube-wells in the village. Wind blowing from north to south direction is affecting crop since last 10 years, especially cauliflower and mustard. Soil in the village is do moth and water is normal. Wheat is the main crop while paddy was introduced around six years back. Vegetable is cultivated in large quantity in this village with availability of water and market nearby.

Such cultivation is constrained by irregular electricity, crop disease, pest attacks and pollution. Blue bull is a threat to guava, cauliflower and horse gram. They eat away the tips of the vegetables and the tender leaves of the guava trees. Spinach leaves face pollution from Ballabhgarh with a thin layer of smoke around. The village cultivates carrot, okra, radish, cauliflower, brinjal, spinach and potato.

Sahapur Kalan

Village Sahapur Kalan is located near village Chandawali and Sohtai. Ballabhgarh is 10 km away and Faridabad town is at a distance of 17 km. There are 168 households in the village with population of 1699 and 850 voters. The different castes residing in the village are Brahmin, Rajput, Potter and Dalit. This village is dominated by Brahmin and many Brahmin and Rajput households are into agriculture-related activities as compared to a few households from other castes. Livelihoods of people depend on land, livestock, labour and salaried job. Around 70 per cent are involved in land cultivation and livestock rearing.

Soil pattern is muddy and water availability is normal. Nearly 150 acres of land in the village is irrigated by Agra canal. A few years ago, polluted water from the canal damaged crops. There are 30 tractors and 50 tube-wells in the village. People from this village go to Ballabhgarh for work. In this village sugarcane cultivation has been stopped since 30 years due to damage to crop by blue bulls. There are no factories inside the village. Many households in the village have started cultivating paddy. In this village cultivation of vegetables is relatively less because the blue bulls tend to destroy the crop. Apart from that, the polluted water damages the crop. If stranded in water people start to get severe itching and swelling in legs and hands. The polluted water is allergic and breeding ground of mosquitoes. The soil of the area has become black due to black water. The polluted water flows through six villages including Chandawali, another vegetable producing village.

Annex 3

PROFILE OF STUDY VILLAGES IN PERI-URBAN—VARANASI

Peri-urban villages: Lohta, Bharthara, Maraw, Parampur, Sundernagar and Chandpur

Lohta

Village Lohta is counted amongst the few spinach cultivating villages. Spinach is grown here extensively throughout the year. In addition to spinach, cultivators grow cauliflowers also. Lohta is also famous for Bananasi sari weaving. All caste groups—Muslims, Moryas, Patels—are engaged in sari weaving. It has become one of the main livelihoods in this village. Lohta is a peri-urban area, situated on the Varanasi-Bhadohi national highway. It is seven km west from Varanasi cantonment—GT road. The village is located about four km from the block headquarter, Kashi Vidyapith. It is surrounded by the villages Mehmudpur in the north, Haralpalpur in the south, Chandapur in the east and Dhanipur in the west. Being roadside location, the village is extremely congested with various types of shops, telephone booths, vegetable katra, wholesale market for fruit and vegetable, wholesale and retail market for silk saris. The villagers told that the urbanization was very rapid during the past hence the price of the land has hiked. Many villagers have sold their land because of high returns and started business. The village is exposed to severe vehicular pollution, traffic-dust and excess garbage due to dense population.

During group discussion, a woman participant commented, "We are annoyed with our neighbours. They use to throw garbage in our agricultural land. This has caused a massive reduction in the yield". Our cultivation is affected a lot and yield has been reducing because our neighbours throw domestic garbage on our cultivated land.

The village has a very interesting past. The father of the former Pradhan, Shree Ram Maurya, was one of the Durbari of Kashi Naresh. In 1942, the inhabitant of Lohta participated in the *freedom struggle*: *Karo or Maro* ("do or die").

The village was exposed to Hindu-Muslim riots in 1948 and 1992. In 1992 during Ayodhaya–Babri riot, 22 villagers were murdered. The inhabitants are the original residents of Lohta. In this village the main caste groups are: Morya, Patel, Muslims, Dalit, Vaishya, washermen and blacksmith. Earlier, almost all houses were clay built, but now almost 80 per cent have been cemented. The village road-Kharanja is brick built. The villagers hope for a major change in the village in the coming years. The cultivation will come down because people will shift to various occupations. The literacy rate will improve. The village will be more prosperous. There are five hamlets in the village. These hamlets are as follows:

- Morya hamlet
- Muslim hamlet
- Dalit hamlet
- Patel hamlet
- Vaishya hamlet

The total population of the village is 28,000 people with 15,401 males and 12,599 females. The total HH number is 4,309. The main caste groups are Brahmin, Muslim, Morya, Vaisya, Nonia, Patel, Barber, washerman, Lohar and Dalit. The main livelihoods in the village are agriculture, vegetable cultivation, daily wage earnings, barber, shopping, government and private service, sari weavings. The number and percentage of HH in various occupational groups are as follows:

• Cultivation	397 HH	9.21 per cent
• Vegetable cultivation	94 HH	2.18 per cent
• Daily wage earner	722 HH	16.75 per cent
• Barber	3 HH	0.07 per cent
• Shopping	110 HH	2.55 per cent
• Government service	11 HH	0.25 per cent
• Sari weaving	4107 HH	95.31 per cent
• Private service	47 HH	1.09 per cent

The literacy rate of the village is 70 per cent for the males and only 30 per cent for the females.

The total area of the village is 450 acres, out of which 383 acres is habited (85.11 % of the land) and 67 acres (14.89%) is cultivable. Cauliflower is cultivated in one acre only (1.49 % of the land). Spinach is cultivated in three acres (4.48 %) of the land. There is electricity in the village. There are schools in the village, both private and government. The village is equipped with urban facilities — post office, marketing, health care facility-private nursing home, clinics as well as government health care centers, cinema hall, telephone booths etc. Drinking water facility is there — supply water, well and hand pump. There are private pump sets.

Bharthara

The village is located 6 km from the block headquarter, Kashi Vidyapith. It is an interior villages, about two km from the very busy Varanasi-Bhadohi Road. The distance from the block-headquarter is 6 km. The GT Road is about 4 km. The surrounding villages are Dindayalpur in the north, Lohta in the south, Phulwaria in the east and Dhamapur in the west. In the district, the name of Bharthara is very famous for cauliflower supply in the main wholesales as well as retail markets in Varanasi district. All six varieties of cauliflower—Kuari, Katki, Aghani, Poosi, Maghi and Sonobal—are produced here. In addition, spinach is also cultivated in the village when we visited the village we found spinach was ready and being sold in the market.

The people of Bharthara are still traditional in caring their agricultural land. The charge of one day, the villagers told, was Rs. 300 plus the food arrangement of 6 persons for two days. The inhabitants of the village are the original inhabitants. The villagers remember that the village was founded around 17th century and that they are the seventh generation of the original founders. The village was under the kingdom or Ramnagar. The village has been named after Bharateshwar God, whose temple is on the west. In 1942, the river Varuna flooded the village. Even now the village is exposed to frequent floods. The oldest man of the village is Laxmi Kant Mishra, who is 85 years old.

The villagers believe that the cultivation was shrinking very rapidly. The main reason is acute shortage of water. The irrigation network, which was constructed with the government tubewell, has been damaged. The villagers no longer use this. The villagers feel that the canals were damaged due to the brick kiln, which was on the eastern side of the village. In the process of preparation of bricks the soil near the canal was denuded.

The *Chakbandi* has been done in the village in the 1995-96. There are seven hamlets in the village are as follows:

- Morya
- Pal
- Patel
- Dalit
- Brahmin

- Yadav
- Vedawali

Out of the above hamlets, five hamlets are horticulture producers, and all are consumers of vegetables. These are Morya, Pal, Patel, Yadav and Bedavali. The total population of the village is 5600 persons with 3119 (55.69 %) males and 2481 (44.30 %) females.

The total HH is 369. The total women headed households (WHH) are 13 (3.52%). The main caste groups are Brahmin, Bhumihars, Yadav, Dalit, Morya, Gararia, etc. The main livelihoods in the village are agriculture, vegetable cultivation, daily wage earners, dairy business, contractor, service, shopping, sari weaving. The number and percentage of HH in various occupational groups are as follows:

• Cultivation	336 HH	91.06 per cent
• Vegetable cultivation	203 HH	55.01 per cent
• Daily wage earner	149 HH	40.38 per cent
• Dairy	25 HH	6.77 per cent
• Contractor	9 HH	2.44 per cent
• Government service	38 HH	10.30 per cent
• Private service	79 HH	21.41 per cent
• Business	3 HH	0.81 per cent
• Shop owner	29 HH	7.86 per cent

The literacy rate of the village is 60 per cent for the males and only 40 per cent for the females.

The total area of the village is 900 acres, out of which 22 acres is habited (2.44% of the land) and 878 acres (97.56%) of the land is cultivable. Cauliflower is cultivated in 79 acres (9.08 %) of the land. Okra is cultivated on 6 (0.68 %) acres of land. Spinach is cultivated in 20 acres (2.28 %) of the land.

• Landless	53 HH	14.36 per cent
• Below 2 acres	225 HH	69.10 per cent
• 2 to 4 acres	46 HH	12.47 per cent
• 4 to 6 acres	10 HH	2.71 per cent
• 6 to 8 acres	5 HH	1.35 per cent

There is electricity in the village. The road inside the village is both kachcha and pucca. There is government primary school. There are wells and hand pumps for drinking water. Private pump sets are there for irrigation. There is neither post office nor health care facilities within the village.

Maraw

The village Maraw is a large village in Kashi Vidyapith block. The vegetable cultivating area is very large. Acres of land are covered with cauliflower. The cultivators cultivate both cauliflower and spinach in the same land. The DLW (Diesel Locomotive Works, Manduadih), Market is the market of Maraw village. Many cultivators—men, women and adolescents sell their vegetables daily in on retail basis. The village is located 2 kms inside, west to the GT Road. The railway line Varanasi-Allahabad crosses the village. It is surrounded by the villages Bhulanpur in the north, Paharigaon in the south, Jalalipatti in the east and Jafarabad in the west.

The village has an interesting past. It is a very old village. It existed on 1885 or earlier than that. The village was named Maraw after the name of a person Madhavi Prasad, who was a famous person. The people of Maraw are the fifth generation of Madhavi Prasad. The villagers worship Dih Baba as God. They sacrificed goat in order to please him so that yield of crop is good. Currently, this practice does not exist. There are two memorable incidences in the village. In 1967, the crop of the village was damaged totally resulting in a severe famine. In 1945, the whole village was affected by plague. People evacuated their houses and lived under the open sky.

Previously most of the houses were clay-built which are remodelled to brick/cemented.

The villagers want to remodel their village and make it a model village. They want pucca road, drainage facilities, uninterrupted electricity supply, primary, middle and high school, health care centre with good doctors and nurses and irrigation facility by the government (pump sets). There are 12 hamlets in the village are as follows:

- Patel hamlet
- Yadav hamlet
- Morya hamlet
- Dalit hamlet
- Pal hamlet
- Rajbhar hamlet
- Maraw Bolia
- Dalgaria pura
- Nai basti
- Thakur basti
- Mushar tola
- Kumhar tola

The total population of the village is 3115 with 1692 males and 1423 females. The total HHs are 326. The total women headed households (WHHs) are 23. The main caste groups are Bhumihar, Brahmins, Backward (Morya, Patel, Barber, Yadav) and Scheduled Castes (Dalits, Mushars, Kumhar, etc). The main livelihoods of the village are agriculture, vegetable cultivation, daily wage earners, weavers, and contractors. A few villagers are engaged in milk business and artificial *motimala* (bead necklace) preparation. The number and percentage of HH in various occupational groups are given below:

• Cultivation	232 HH	71.16 per cent
• Vegetable cultivation	232 HH	71.16 per cent
• Daily wage earner	97 HH	29.75 per cent
• Dairy	7 HH	2.15 per cent
• Contractor	10 HH	3.07 per cent
• Service	44 HH	13.50 per cent
• Sari weaving	43 HH	13.19 per cent
• Moti-Mala	10 HH	3.07 per cent

The literacy rate of the village is 70 per cent for the males and only 30 per cent for the females.

The total area of the village is 441 acres, out of which 47 acres is inhabited (10.66% of the land) and 394 acres (89.34%) is cultivable land. Cauliflower is cultivated in 113 acres (28.68%) of the land. Okra is cultivated in 9 acres (2.28%) of the land. Spinach is cultivated in 17 acres (4.31%) of the land.

• Low economic status	95 HH-	29.14 per cent
• Medium economic status	225 HH-	69.02 per cent
• High economic status	6 HH-	1.84 per cent

The pattern of land holdings in the village is as follows:

• Below20 acres	93 HH-	29.14 per cent
• 20 to 4 acres	227 HH-	69.63 per cent
• 4 to 6 acres	1 HH-	0.31 per cent
• 8 acres and above	5 HH-	1.53 per cent

Amongst infrastructure there is electricity in the village. There is private school but no government school. The road inside the village is both kuchcha and pucca. There is no post office and health care centre. For drinking water facility, there are the wells and hand pumps. There is no pipe line water facility in the village.

Parampur

The village Parampur is one of the few villages where okra is cultivated extensively in a very large land area. The okra cultivation yields income continuously for eight months. After harvesting about six months, the cultivator cuts the stem, which again starts yield after 15 days and continues for about two months. The cultivators plant turai in okra plants. The village is very famous in Varanasi district and in the *Chanua satti* (whole sale market) for intensive okra supply. Okra is one of the main vegetables of Parampur, which caters to the demand of Allahabad, Kanpur, Kolkata and such other places.

The village Parampur is situated on the Varanasi-Bhadohi national highway. It is about 13 km west of the Varanasi cantonment and 6 km south-west of the block Arajilines, 10 km from the very busy GT Road.The surrounding villages are Sajoai in the north, Naraicha in the south, Ramraipur in the east and Kuraona in the west. It is believed that the village was founded in sixteenth century, with the arrival of a villager from Bhadohi, named Surai. He had a clash with Brahmins and fled to this area. Rajbhars are his descendents. It is the fifth generation of Rajbhars.

There are two hamlets in the village — Rajbhar and Bangala. The total population of the village is 1600 persons, with 860 (53.75 %) males and 740 (46.25 %) females. The total number of HHs is 188, with 10 women headed households. The main caste groups are Rajbhar, Morya, Patel, etc. The main livelihood of the village is cultivation (188 HHs), vegetable cultivation (188 HHs), sari weaving (50 HHs), and daily wage earners (48 HHs).

The proportions of households pursuing main livelihoods are as follows:

- Cultivation (188 HHs) 100 per cent
- Vegetable cultivation (188 HHs) 100 per cent
- Daily wage earners (48 HHs) 25.53 per cent
- Sari weaving (50 HHs) 26.59 per cent

The literacy rate of the village is 60 per cent for the males and only 40 per cent for the females. The total area of the village is 500 acres, of which 324 acres is inhabited and 176 acres is cultivable land. Out of 176 acres, ladyfinger is cultivated in 53 acres (30.11 %), spinach in 9 (5.11 %) acres and cauliflower in one acre (0.57 %). The socio-economic groups in the village are as follows:

- Low economic status 82 HHs 43.62 per cent
- Medium economic status 98 HHs 52.13 per cent
- High economic status 8 HHs 4.25 per cent

Pattern of land holdings in village Parampur is indicated below:

• Landless	1 HH	0.53 per cent
• Upto 2 acres	179 HHs	95.21 per cent
• 2 acres-4 acres	8 HHs	4.25 per cent

There is electricity in the village and it is connected to the national highway. There is a government primary school in the village. There is government tube well, which is used by the Rajbhar inhabitant. Some villagers in both hamlets have private pump sets. The villagers have own wells and there are hand pumps in the village for drinking water. There is no supply water facility. The road of the village is *kachcha* as well as *pucca.*

The village does not have some basic facilities in its own area.The local post office is in Gangapur village, two km from the village. There is no health care facility in the village. However, there is health sub-centre in neighbouring Narona village, which is located in the south of the village. There are private practitioners in the villages about half km away—Akelwa chouraha and Devta pokhra chouraha.

REFERENCES

Development Tracks RTC (2003): Livelihoods Scoping in West Bengal—Draft Report submitted to DFID, India, April.

Development Tracks RTC (2003): Food Safety, Agriculture and Peri-Urban Areas–Draft Research Report on field study submitted to Imperial College of Science, Technology and Medicine, February.

Development Tracks RTC (2001): Agriculture and Air Pollution in Peri-Urban Areas–Draft Research Report submitted to Imperial College of Science, Technology and Medicine, UK and International Institute for Environment and Development, London, March.

Diana Cartney (1998): *Sustainable Rural Livelihoods – What contribution can we make*? DFID, London.

DFID–See web site www.livelihoods.org

Johnson, H. and G. Wilson (1996): 'Performance, learning and sustaining development management for sustainable development,' DPP Working Paper No. 39, Milton Keynes, The Open University, pp.17-18.

Johnson, H and G. Wilson, 'Institutional sustainability as learning', in Eade Deborah (2000), *Development and Management, Selected essays from Development in Practice*, Introduction by Tina Wallace, Oxfam GB in association with The Open University, p. 70.

Mukherjee, Neela, Meera Jayaswal, *et al.* (2001): *Alternative Perspectives on Livelihoods, Agriculture and Air Pollution, Agriculture in urban and peri-urban areas in a developing country*, SOAS Studies in Development Geography, Ashgate Publishing Co., U.K and Concept Publishing Co., New Delhi.

Mukherjee, Amitava (2002): *Perspectives of the Silent Majority: Air Pollution, Livelihood and Food Security*, SOAS Studies in Development Geography, Ashgate Publishing Co., U.K and Concept Publishing Co., New Delhi.

Mukherjee, Neela (2002): *Participatory Learning and Action with 100 Field Methods*, Concept Publishing Co., New Delhi.

Mukherjee, Neela (1993): *Participatory Rural Appraisal: Methodology and Applications*, Concept Publishing Co., New Delhi.

Mukherjee, Neela (1997): *Participatory Appraisal of Natural Resources*, Concept Publishing Co., New Delhi.

Mukherjee, Neela (1995): *Questionnaire Survey and Participatory Rural Appraisal*, Concept Publishing Co., New Delhi, 1995.

Mukherjee, Neela *et al.* (2001): Air Pollution, Farming Systems and Livelihoods in Peri-Urban Areas–Evidence from Haryana, *Economic and Political Weekly*, February 17.

INDEX